Make Sausages Great Again

Stanley Marianski, Adam Marianski

Bookmagic LLC
Seminole, Florida

Make Sausages Great Again
Stanley Marianski, Adam Marianski

ISBN: 978-0-9904586-8-5

Bookmagic, LLC.
http://www.bookmagic.com

Printed in the United States of America.

Contents

Introduction

Why Make Sausages at Home? Well, the answer is very simple: you cannot find them anymore. Do not confuse a minced and spiced meat that is stuffed into a casing and ends up on a grill with a great sausage. Or a mass-produced product which has only the looks of the sausage, but not the taste or flavor. The era of buying quality sausages is ending fast. To get a great sausage one must buy one that carries European certificate of origin, buy a sausage from a dwindling number of remaining European stores or make one for themselves.

Sausage making knowledge originated in Europe and was brought to the USA by immigrants in the last century. German, Polish and Italian butcher shops were in every major city and offered a variety of wonderful meats and sausages. Most of the great sausage making stores located in large cities like New York were profitable because the immigrant sausage makers bought the buildings when the prices were low. So, they didn't have to worry about paying the rent. A local sausage maker supplied the whole neighborhood with quality products and he did not need to compete with the large supermarkets which carried a limited selection of sausages.

Those original butchers are a dying breed today and their sons and daughters do not want to continue the family tradition. They do not want to get up at 3 o'clock in the morning to start their work day. They inherited the business and sold the buildings at a profit or rented the stores out. As a result, many sausage making facilities cease to exist. This trend is not limited to the USA but happens in Germany, Spain and in other countries.

In Europe you could not just open a sausage making business because it seemed a good idea. You had to complete the required curriculum and then learn the trade by working as an apprentice in an established sausage making shop. In American cities many sausage making shops were sold by the originally trained European butchers to people who looked for an investment opportunity. The new owners continued to make simple sausages, but bought more difficult ones from large producers at wholesale prices.

In the USA there are no questions about what you know about nitrates, curing meat, safety procedures, or the like. All you need is to rent a place, the easiest way is to buy an established place that conforms to minimum food safety standards, buy equipment and start making sausages. A person sold a contracting business in Chicago, moved to Florida and bought a sausage making kitchen from the owner who was getting too old to run it. The irony is that the owner hardly knew what he was doing himself. Another guy got tired of cutting meat in a supermarket so he bought a grocery store with a little kitchen in the back and started making sausages. Those stores may carry a fresh grilled type sausage, one or two smoked sausages, but sausages such as liver sausages, head cheeses or salami are bought at wholesale price from more established producers.

The large meat processors that supply supermarkets carry a lot of blame. Here the entire strategy is based on increasing profits in order to satisfy the company's shareholders. Those mass-produced sausages contain countless additives and ingredients to make sausages look pretty and last for as long as possible, otherwise supermarkets will not renew the order.

Fortunately, anybody who learns the basics can make great sausages at home. This book loaded with rules and tips will guide the reader all the way. I have written a number of more complete and large books on this subject, but have challenged myself to writing a smaller book that can compile the maximum amount of knowledge into fewer pages. And I only wish today that such a book existed when I started making sausages. The book will help the reader to make safe products and avoid mistakes that would have been otherwise made. By studying this book anybody can become an accomplished sausage maker and make some great products.

Stanley Marianski
December 2020

Chapter 1

Safety, Nitrates and Curing Meat

Why Make Sausages?

Because there aren't many quality sausages left around. To get a top quality sausage sausage you need to:

- find a meat store that was established by a professionally trained sausage maker from Europe and hope that he passed his skills to someone else.
- buy quality products online. The best sausages carry the European Certificate of Origin, however, most of them are available only in Europe.
- make sausages yourself.

Why Can You Make Better Sausages than a Commercial Producer?

Because: **1.** you can select better meat, **2.** you don't need to deal with supermarkets, **3.** you don't need to pump meat with water, **4.** you don't need to use chemicals, **5.** you can create a new recipe at will and you are in full control.

1. Good meat makes a good sausage. Commercial producers cannot afford to use high quality meats because they produce sausages to make money, they don't do it for pleasure. Every meat cut, fat, offal meat, skins, including machine scraped meat from bones is utilized to save money in order to come up with the lowest price. And that translates into higher profits for shareholders.

2. As long as the supermarket renews the order everybody is happy. A supermarket does not need a superior quality product that is made without chemicals because it will have a short shelf life. A supermarket wants a sausage that last for weeks or months. Sliced sausage must retain its original color in spite of being continuously bombarded with fluorescent light. After a few months the fat develops rancidity (off flavor) which must be prevented. All those technical problems are solved by introducing special additives and chemicals to extend the life of the product. This gives the supermarket more time to sell it. And when the expiration date becomes dangerously close the supermarket uses the magical trick: "buy one, get one free" and the product is sold.

3. A terrible practice is pumping water into meat. Although an enormous amount of sausages are sold in the USA, there is one type of sausage that gets most of the credit for sales. And this is an emulsified sausage: hot dog, wiener, frankfurter or bologna. In order to produce emulsified paste the meat must be very finely chopped in bowl cutters. As the bowl turns slowly around a set of sharp round knives placed above cut the meat by rotating thousands of times per minute.

The resulting friction will dull the knives and will cook the meat so in order to protect the equipment a "certain" amount of crushed ice or icy cold water is introduced to lower the temperature. In order to prevent this water from leaking out "phosphates" are added and the water is locked inside the meat. If only 10% ice is added, that would be fine, however, "phosphates" can bind even 50% of water. This is the reason why mass-produced frankfurters are made so cheaply as the customer is buying water without knowing it.

Adding water *dilutes the flavor* of the meat – add water to soup or tea and see the difference. Except the shape those sausages have nothing in common with frankfurters or other emulsified sausages which were originally produced from pork and veal. The difference in taste and flavor is like the difference between night and the day.

4. Sausages do not need chemicals, the meat, salt, spices and time is all that is needed.

5. A hobbyist can create or change a recipe in an instant. He can improvise and introduce new ingredients that he likes, his imagination is the limit to the number of recipes he can create. A meat plant cannot afford to take a risk of making sausages with blueberries and supermarket will be hesitant to order it. The moral of the story is simple: a hobbyist can make a better sausage than a commercial plant. It may not look as pretty, meat particles may not be cut so cleanly, but the sausage will have a better taste and be healthier.

Food Safety and Meat Microbiology

Meat of a healthy animal is clean and contains very few bacteria. Any invading bacteria will be destroyed by the animal's immune system. Once the animal is slaughtered these defense mechanisms are destroyed and the meat tissue is subjected to rapid decay. Although unaware of the process, early sausage makers knew that once the animal was killed it was a race between external preservation techniques and the decomposition of the raw meats.

Most bacteria are present on the skin and in the intestines. In a stressed animal bacteria are able to travel from the animal's gut right through the casing into the meat. The slaughtering process starts introducing bacteria into the exposed surfaces. Given time they will find their way inside anyhow, but the real trouble starts when *we* create a new surface cut with a knife. This creates an opening for bacteria to enter the meat from the outside and start spoiling it. We must realize that they don't appear in some magical way inside of the meat, they always start from *the outside and they work their way in.*

Fig. 1.1 Relationship between meat surface area and volume.

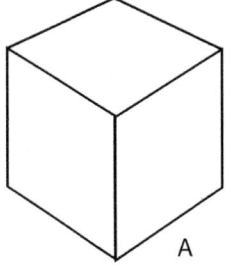
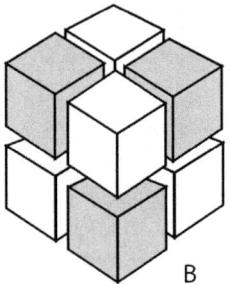

A. Cube A is 1 inch on each side and has a volume of 1 cubic inch and the surface area of 6 square inches. **B.** Three complete cuts (two vertical and one horizontal) produce eight small cubes with a volume of 0.125 cubic inch. Total *volume remains the same -* 1 cubic inch, but total *surface area has doubled* and is 12 square inches.

This is what happens when the meat is cut, the surface area increases. Now imagine what happens when the grinder cuts meat through a 1/8" (3 mm) plate, it creates an infinite number of small particles. The more cuts, the more spoils of meat, the more air and free water available to bacteria. This is the reason why *ground meat has the shortest shelf life*. In a large piece of meat the outside surface serves as a natural barrier preventing access to bacteria. *They have a long distance to travel to reach the center of the meat.*

Meat muscles are surrounded with a connective tissue which also *acts as a protective sheath and so does the outside skin*. Duties like cutting meat, grinding, mixing or stuffing all increase meat temperature and should be performed in the kitchen at the lowest possible temperatures as fast as possible. Otherwise we create conditions for the growth of bacteria and that will decrease the shelf life of the product.

All About Bacteria

Food safety is nothing else but the control of bacteria and to do it effectively first we have to learn how bacteria behave. Let's make something clear: it is impossible to eliminate bacteria altogether, life on the planet will come to a halt. They are everywhere: on the floor, on walls, in the air, on our hands and all they need to grow is *moisture, nutrients and warm temperature.*

Meat contains about 75% of water and this moisture is the main reason that it spoils. Bacteria love temperatures that revolve around the temperature of our body 36.6° C (98.6° F). Holding products at higher temperatures (greater than 54° C (130° F) restricts the growth of bacteria. Increasing temperatures over 60° C (140° F) will start killing them. All of them hate cold, and around 0° C (32° F) they become lethargic and dormant when the temperature drops lower. *Keeping them at low temperatures does not kill them, but only stops them from multiplying*. Once when the conditions are favorable again, they will wake up and start growing again.

Given favorable conditions bacteria can double up in numbers every 20 minutes. In a refrigerator their number will also grow, albeit at a reduced pace, but they can double up in 12 hours. Under the correct conditions, spoilage bacteria reproduce rapidly and the populations can grow very large. Temperature and time are the factors that affect bacterial growth the most. Below 7° C (45° F) bacteria grow slowly and at temperatures above 60° C (140° F) they start to die. In the so called "danger zone" between 40-140° F (4-60° C) many bacteria grow very well. When bacteria grow, they increase in numbers, not in size.

After cooking, meats are free of bacteria, but leaving them warm for an extended time *will invite new bacteria* to settle in and start growing. For this reason smoked and subsequently cooked meats are submitted to cold showers to pass through the "danger zone" as fast as possible.

Microorganisms which are of special interest when processing meats:
- Food spoilage bacteria.
- Dangerous (pathogenic) bacteria.
- Beneficial bacteria.
- Yeasts and molds.

Spoilage bacteria break down meat proteins and fats causing food to deteriorate and develop unpleasant odors, tastes, and textures. Fruits and vegetables get mushy or slimy and meat develops a bad odor. Most people would not eat spoiled food. However, if they did, they probably would not get seriously sick. Bacteria such as *Pseudomonas spp.* or *Brochotrix thermosphacta* cause slime, discoloration and odors, but don't produce toxins.

Pathogenic bacteria cause illness. They grow rapidly in the "danger zone" - the temperatures between 5-60° C (40-140° F) - and *do not generally affect the taste, smell, or appearance of food.* Food that is left too long at warm temperatures could be dangerous to eat, but smell and look just fine. *Clostridium botulinum, Bacillus cereus* or *Staphylococcus aureus* infect food with toxin which will bring harm to us in just a few hours. Others like *Salmonella* or *Escherichia coli* will find their way with infected meat into our intestines, and *if present in sufficient numbers*, will pose a serious danger. Pathogenic bacteria hate cold conditions and lie dormant at low temperatures waiting for an opportunity to jump into action when the conditions get warmer again.

Beneficial bacteria make the production of fermented sausages possible. They are naturally occurring in meat but in most cases they are added into the meat in the form of starter cultures. There are two classes of beneficial (friendly) bacteria:
- Lactic acid producing bacteria - *Lactobacillus, Pediococcus.*
- Color and flavor forming bacteria - *Staphylococcus, Kocuria* (previously known as *Micrococcus*).

Yeasts and molds grow much slower than bacteria and they develop later in the drying process. In European fermented sausages, the development of mold is often seen as a desired feature as it contributes to the mellower flavor of the sausage. Yeasts need little oxygen to survive, and live on the surface or near the surface inside of the sausage. Molds need oxygen and will grow on the surface of the sausage only

What is Botulism?

Botulism is a rare but serious food borne disease. Sausages are the second biggest source of food contamination and food poisoning, second only to home-canned food products. The symptoms of botulism include difficulty swallowing, talking, breathing, and double vision. Without medical care, respiratory failure and death are likely. Botulism symptoms typically appear within 18 to 36 hours of eating the contaminated food, although it can be as soon as four hours and last up to eight days. The optimal temperature range for the growth of botulinum bacteria is 26-35° C (78-95° F) and it significantly slows down at 48° C (118° F). When these bacteria feel threatened, they envelop themselves in protective shells called "spores" which can only be killed by boiling at 100° C (212° F) or at 115° C (240° F) for at least 10 minutes.

At 60° C (140° F) botulinum spores do not develop into toxins, although they are heat resistant.

Where Does Botulism Come From?

Clostridium botulinum is found in soil and aquatic sediments all over the world. Like plant seeds, they can lie dormant for years. They are not threatening until they encounter an adequate environment for growth. The spores that germinate produce the deadly botulinum toxin. To grow, they require a slightly acidic, oxygen free environment that is warm and moist. That is exactly what happens when smoking meats:

1. Meats contain a lot of moisture. Water is then also added to sausages to facilitate stuffing. Hams and other meats are pumped with water.

2. Lack of oxygen – when smoking we intentionally decrease the amount of available air. This allows our sawdust or wood chips to generate lots of smoke.

3. Temperatures between 5-60° C (40-140° F) - much smoking is done at this temperature range. The most dangerous range is from 26-35° C (78-95° F), and that fits into the "warm smoking" method. Bacteria thrive at this temperature range and the smoking process creates ideal conditions for *Cl. botulinum* to grow.

How to Prevent Botulism

The answer lies in the use of *nitrates/nitrites*. When present, they prevent the transformation of *Cl. botulinum* spores into toxins. It is almost like applying a vaccine to eliminate a disease. By curing meats with nitrites, we protect ourselves from possibly contracting a deadly disease. Nitrites are cheap, commonly available, and completely safe in amounts recommended by the Food and Drug Administration. So why not use them? All commercial plants do. Nitrites are needed only when smoking meats or making fermented sausages. You don't need nitrites when barbecuing or grilling, as the temperatures are high enough to inhibit the development of botulinum spores into toxins.

Trichinae

There are some cold smoked pork products and sausages that will not be submitted to the cooking process and they can be at risk of being infected with trichinae. Trichinae is an illness caused by the consumption of raw or under cooked pork or wild game meat infected with *"trichinella spiralis."* Deers are herbivores; they eat leaves from trees, bushes and shrubs and they don't contract the disease. Trichinae is a parasitic nematode (round worm) that can migrate from the digestive tract and settle in the form of cysts in various muscles of the body. The disease is almost non-existent in American pigs due to their strictly controlled feed, but it can still be found in meats of free roaming animals. The illness is not contagious, but the first symptoms appear within 1-2 days of eating contaminated meat. They include nausea, diarrhea, vomiting, abdominal pain, itchy skin, and may be mistaken for the flu. Trichinae in pork is killed by raising its internal temperature to 58° C (137° F). The U.S. Code of Federal Regulations requires pork to be cooked for 1 minute at 60° C (140° F). Traditionally made fermented sausages, also called dry or slow-fermented sausages are normally never cooked and the heat treatment does not apply here.

They are cured with a higher percentage of salt which kills *trichinae* too. Fortunately, *storing pork at low temperatures also kills trichinae*. The U.S. Department of Agriculture's Code of Federal Regulations, Title 9, Volume 2, Cite: 9 CFR318.10 requires that pork intended for use in processed products be frozen at:

Group 1 - comprises product in separate pieces not exceeding 6" (15 cm) in thickness, or arranged on separate racks with layers not exceeding 6" (15 cm) in depth, or stored in crates or boxes not exceeding 6" (15 cm) in depth, or stored as solidly frozen blocks not exceeding 6" (15 cm) in thickness.

Group 2 - comprises product in pieces, layers, or within containers, the thickness of which exceeds 6" (15 cm) but not 27" (68 cm) and product in containers including tierces, barrels, kegs, and cartons having a thickness not exceeding 27" (68 cm).

Table 1. Required Period of Freezing Indicated			
Temperature		Days	
° F	° C	Group 1	Group 2
5	-15	20	30
- 10	-23.3	10	20
- 20	-28.9	6	12

The product undergoing such refrigeration or the containers thereof shall be so spaced while in the freezer as will insure a free circulation of air between the pieces of meat, layers, blocks, boxes, barrels, and tierces in order that the temperature of the meat throughout will be promptly reduced to not higher than 5° F (-15° C), -10° F (-23.3° C), or -20° F (-28.9° C), as the case may be (check the above table). Microwaving, curing, drying or smoking is not effective in preventing Trichinae. It should be noted that *freezing will not kill larval cysts in bears and other wild game that live in Northwestern U.S. and Alaska.* That meat has to be cooked to 72° C (160° F) internal temperature.

Trichinae Control in Dry Meat Products

Pork products which are not cooked such as slow fermented and dried sausages are at risk of being infected with *trichinae*. Cured hams and butts fit into the same category and must be dealt with differently. Although it is possible to obtain certified pork trichinae free it is not something that is universally done as it requires laboratory tests. Curing meats with salt according to USDA regulations takes care of the problem. Hams were cured with salt long before the USDA came to be and the procedures used in the past took care of the trichinae problem.

As explained earlier freezing pork meat is an approved method for treating trichinae and it can be applied at home. It is not practical for large scale production as it will require an investment in time and space plus additional electricity costs. In addition frozen meat exhibits damaged cell structure due to the growth of ice crystals. That will affect the texture and sliceability of the finished ham. The best solution is to use enough salt that will remove moisture, slow the growth of bacteria and will eliminate the *trichinae* problem.

Most prescribed procedures call for 3.3% salt for dry sausages and 4-5% salt for large whole meats like shoulders and hams. Those amounts which are usually applied anyhow, will cure meats and treat them for *trichinae* at the same time. There are detailed USDA instructions on preventing *trichinae* by curing pork with salt. Keep in mind that pork that comes from unverified sources and use in *fermented spreadable sausages* should be treated for *trichinae* by freezing.

Good Manufacturing Practices that Can be Applied in the Everyday Kitchen

Home made sausages are subject to the ambient temperature of the kitchen and a dose of common sense is of invaluable help:

- Take only what you need from the cooler.
- When a part of the meat is processed put it back into the cooler.
- Keep your equipment clean and cold.
- Work as fast as possible.
- Try to always keep meat refrigerated.
- If your premises are not temperature controlled, limit your production to late evening or early morning hours.
- Wash your hands often.

The presented hurdles increase our defense against the growth of bacteria and by implementing those simple recommendations we greatly increase our chances for producing quality sausages.

Temperature Control

If you live in a tropical climate without air conditioning, try to process meat in the evening or early morning hours and work with a small portion of meat at one time. Other factors which influence your product quality and can eliminate the danger of any food poisoning are the 4 C's of Food Hygiene:

- Cleanliness-wash hands, prevent insects, use clean equipment.
- Cooking-cook meat, poultry and fish to proper internal temperature.
- Chilling and storage-keep food at refrigerator temperature.
- Cross-contamination-don't mix raw and cooked meats, use clean knives, keep separate cutting boards for cooked and raw meat.

Nitrates

Nitrates in food is a misunderstood topic that scares many, though nitrates play an important role in fighting bacteria and preserving meat. Nitrates were not invented by modern science, they were discovered by our ancestors thousands of years ago.

Rock salts were mined in different parts of the world and exhibited different properties that were caused mainly by impurities contained within. Take for example Himalayan salt that is intended for cooking - it is pink. In the past when we used salt with a higher potassium nitrate content, we discovered that the meat had a different taste and color.

The Chinese invented gunpowder in 9th century and potassium nitrate was the main ingredient for making gun powder. Its commercial name was saltpeter and it is still used today. Potassium Nitrate (KNO3-Bengal saltpetre) or sodium Nitrate (NaNO3-Chile saltpetre) were even added to water causing the temperature to drop and that method was used to cool wine in the XVI century. Who came with idea of treating meat with nitrate we will never know, it is possible that gunpowder was spilled over the meat by an accident. The meat remained red even after cooking and later we discovered more benefits of using nitrate.

Nitrates and nitrites are powerful poisons and that is why the Food and Drug Administration established limits for their use. *So why do we use them?* The simple answer is that after testing and experiments, our modern science has not come up with a better solution to cure meats and prevent food poisoning. Only in the XIX century a German fellow Justinus Kemer linked food poisoning to contaminated sausages. It took another 80 years to discover botulinum bacteria by Emile Pierre van Ermengem, Professor of bacteriology at the University of Ghent in 1895. The first scientific papers that explained the behavior of nitrates were published only in the XX century so why had we been using nitrates so much? Not to prevent botulism of which we had never even heard of before.

We had been and still are using nitrates because:

- Nitrates can preserve meat's natural color. The same piece of ham when roasted will have a light brown color and is known as roasted leg of pork. Add some nitrates to it, cook it and it becomes ham with its characteristic flavor and pink color.
- Nitrates impart a characteristic cured flavor to meat.
- Nitrates prevent the transformation of botulinum spores into toxins thus eliminating the possibility of food poisoning.
- Nitrates prevent rancidity of fats.

Nitrate Safety Concerns

There has been much concern over the consumption of Nitrates by the general public. Studies have shown that when nitrites combine with by-products of protein (amines in the stomach), that leads to the formation of nitrosamines which are carcinogenic (cancer causing) in laboratory animals. There was also a link that when Nitrates were used to cure bacon and the latter one was fried until crispy, it helped to create nitrosamines. In order to accomplish that, the required temperatures had to be in the 315° C (600° F) range. Most meats are smoked and cooked well below 93° C (200° F) so they are not affected. Those findings started a lot of unnecessary panic in the 1970's about the harmful effects of nitrates on our health. Millions of dollars were spent, a lot of research was done, many researchers had spent long sleepless nights seeking fame and glory, but no evidence was found that when nitrates are used within the established limits they can pose any danger to our health.

A review of all scientific literature on nitrite by the National Research Council of the National Academy of Sciences indicates that nitrite does not directly harm us in any way.

All this talk about the danger of nitrite in our meats pales in comparison with the amounts of nitrates that are found in vegetables that we consume every day. The nitrates get to them from the fertilizers which are used in agriculture. Don't blame sausages for the nitrates you consume, blame the farmer. It is more dangerous to one's health to eat vegetables on a regular basis than a sausage. You will notice that in addition to the term potassium *nitrate* another term sodium *nitrite* is used. *Nitrate* was used for hundreds of years but *nitrite* was discovered only about one hundred years ago. They are very similar, when meat bacteria reacts with nitrate a new component called sodium *nitrite* is produced. The meat industry predominantly uses sodium *nitrite* today because it is easier to calculate, it is stronger and can be effective at lower temperatures than nitrate. In the US curing salt is available in two forms:

Cure #1 (also known as Instacure #1, Prague Powder #1 or Pink Cure #1). For any aspiring sausage maker it is a necessity to understand and know how to apply Cure #1 and Cure #2, as those two cures are used worldwide though under different names and with different proportions of nitrates and salt. Cure #1 is a mixture of 1 oz of sodium *nitrite* (6.25%) to 1 lb of salt. It must be used to cure all meats that will require smoking at low temperatures. It is the universally used cure in the USA.

Cure #2 (also known as Instacure #2, Prague Powder #2 or Pink Cure #2). Cure #2 is a mixture of 1 oz of sodium *nitrite* (6.25%) along with 0.64 oz of sodium *nitrate* (4%) to 1 lb of salt. It must be used with any products that do not require cooking, smoking or refrigeration and is *mainly used for products that will be air cured for a long time* like country ham, salami, pepperoni, and other dry sausages. Both Cure #1 and Cure #2 contain a small amount of FDA approved red coloring agent that gives them a slight pink color thus eliminating any possible confusion with common salt and that is why they are sometimes called "pink" curing salts.

European Cures

There are different cures in European countries, for example in Poland a commonly used cure goes by the name "Peklosól" and contains 0.6% of sodium nitrite to salt. No coloring agent is added and it is white in color. In European cures such a low nitrite percentage in salt is self-regulating and it is almost impossible to apply too much nitrite to meat, as the latter will taste too salty. Following a recipe you could replace salt with peklosól altogether and the established nitrite limits will be preserved. This isn't the case with American Cure #1, that contains much more nitrite in it (6.5%) and we have to color it pink to avoid the danger of mistakes and poisoning.

Country	Cure	% of nitrite in salt
USA	Cure #1	6.25
Poland	Peklosól	0.6
Germany	Pökelsalz	0.6
France	Sel nitrité	0.6
Sweden	Colorazo	0.6
England	Nitrited salt	various
Australia	Kuritkwik	various

Comminuted products - small meat pieces, *meat for sausages,* ground meat, poultry etc. Cure #1 was developed in such a way that if we add 4 ounces of Cure #1 to 100 pounds of meat, the quantity of nitrite added to meat will conform to the legal limits (156 ppm) permitted by the Meat Division of the United States Department of Agriculture.

That corresponds to 1 oz. (28.35 g) of Cure #1 for each 25 lb (11.33 kg) of meat or 0.2 oz. (5.66 g) per 5 lb (2.26 kg) of meat.

Comminuted Meat (Sausages)	Cure #1 in ounces	Cure #1 in grams	Cure #1 in teaspoons
25 lbs	1	28.35	5
5 lbs	0.2	5.66	1
1 lb	0.04	1.1	1/5
1 kg	0.08	2.5	1/2

There is no regulatory minimum in-going nitrite level for cured products that have been processed to ensure their shelf stability (such as having undergone a complete thermal process, or having been subjected to adequate pH controls, and/or moisture controls in combination with appropriate packaging). *However, 40-50 ppm nitrite is useful in that it has some preservative effect.* This amount has also been shown to be sufficient for color-fixing purposes and to achieve the expected cured meat or poultry appearance. Some thermally processed shelf-stable (canned) products have a minimum in-going nitrite level that must be monitored because it is specified as a critical factor in the product's process schedule. By the time meats are consumed, they contain less then 50 parts per million of nitrite. It is said that commercially prepared meats in the USA contain about 10 ppm of nitrite when bought in a supermarket. Nitrite and nitrate are not permitted in baby, junior or toddler foods.

Curing Meat

When applied to home made meat products, the term 'curing' usually means *'preserved with salt and nitrite.'* When this term is applied to products made commercially it will mean that meats are prepared with salt, nitrite, ascorbates, erythorbates and dozens more chemicals that are pumped into the meat. There are three curing methods: dry curing, wet curing and combination curing. The dry curing method is used to cure (prepare) meat for making top quality smoked sausages.

Curing Meat for Sausages

Let's make something absolutely clear, you don't need to cure meat to make your sausage. Grind the meat, mix with spices and stuff the mass into a casing. Grill it, hot smoke it, or place it in a refrigerator, the product is still called a sausage. Curing is an extra process that requires more time, designated containers and space in a refrigerator. The reason we advocate the curing procedure is that *this book is about making quality products* and quality takes time. Meat for quality smoked sausage *should be cured.*

Curing imparts a certain peculiar flavor which is in demand by the consumer and if we cure hams, bacon, chops, butts, and fish because they taste better, so why not cure meat for sausages? The fact that we grind meat makes it only easier on our teeth to chew it - it does not improve the color, texture or the flavor of the sausage. Someone might say: but I've mixed nitrite and spices with ground meat before stuffing so that's OK. Well, it's not ok, the problem is that *not enough time* was allocated and the sausage is only partially cured.

Curing procedure

Meat should be cut into smaller pieces, about 2 inches (5-6 cm) and not heavier than 0.5 lb (250 g). Then it is thoroughly mixed with salt, Cure #1 (salt, nitrite), sugar (if used) and packed tightly in a container, not higher than 8 inches (20 cm). Then the meat is covered with a clean cloth and stored in a refrigerator. The cloth prevents oxygen in the air from reacting with sodium nitrite which might weaken the process. In addition there are chemical reactions taking place inside the meat and the cloth allows the gases to evaporate.

The curing times at 4° C (40° F) (refrigerator temperature) are as follows:

•   Meat pieces size 2" - 72 hours.
•   Ground meat - 24 - 36 hours, depending on a particle size.

Photo 11.15 Meats being cured in a cooler.

What will happen to smoked sausages if the meat is not cured? Basically nothing as long as you have added salt and Cure #1 (sodium nitrite) to ground meat. The final color might not be as good as the properly cured sausage but it will still be a good sausage.

Alternative curing methods

If you don't have time or enough space in a refrigerator, use the alternative curing method described below which will develop a red color, however, not given sufficient time they will not be able to develop the curing flavor.

Method 1. Grind each meat through a proper plate (as dictated by the recipe). Salt and sodium nitrite will penetrate tiny pieces of ground meat much faster. Mix meat with salt and Cure #1. Pack tightly (to remove air) and separately, place each type of ground meat in a container and cover it. Let it "set" for 3-4 hours at room temperature 20-22°C (68-71°F). Chemical reactions proceed much faster at higher temperatures and so does curing. Add spices, mix and stuff casings.

Method 2. Grind each meat through a proper plate (as dictated by the recipe). Mix meat with salt, Cure #1 and other ingredients. Stuff sausages and place in a cooler for 12 hours before smoking. When removed from a cooler they have to be conditioned at room temperature for a few hours to remove moisture from the surface.

Method 3. Grind each meat through a proper plate (as dictated by the recipe). Mix meat with salt, Cure #1 and other ingredients. Stuff sausages and hang at room temperature for 2 hours. Transfer to a smokehouse. Apply smoke when sausages feel dry.

As you can see in all instances we are buying extra time for curing to proceed. A commercial producer will not perform curing at higher than cooler temperature as this will affect the shelf life of the product. Commercial processors cure meat faster by using ascorbic acid, erythorbic acid, or their derivatives, sodium ascorbate and/or sodium erythorbate. These additives speed up the chemical conversion of nitrite to nitric oxide which in turn will react with meat myoglobin to create a pink color. They also deplete levels of meat oxygen which prevents the fading of the cured meat color in the presence of light and oxygen.

Those "alternative" curing methods cannot be used when curing whole pieces like hams, butts or loins. Due to the insufficient curing time there will be uneven pink, red or even gray areas inside. That would be easily noticeable when slicing those meats. As sausage is made from comminuted meat any variations in color cannot be spotted, unless larger chunks of meat are added. When making less than 5 pounds of sausage it is perfectly acceptable to make curing a part of the mixing and conditioning process. This way the sausage is stuffed, cured and smoked in one operation.

Curing and Meat Color

The color of *cooked* (uncured) meat varies from greyish brown for beef and grey-white for pork and is due to denaturation (cooking) of *myoglobin*. The color of *cured* meat is pink and is due to the reaction between nitrite and *myoglobin*. The color can vary from light pink to light red and depends on the amount of *myoglobin* a particular meat contains and the amount of nitrite added to the cure. The color of *fresh meat* is determined by the amount of *myoglobin* a particular animal carries. The more *myoglobin* the darker the meat, it is that simple. Going from top to bottom, meats that contain more *myoglobin* are: horse, beef, lamb, veal, pork, poultry and fish. The amount of *myoglobin* present in meat increases with the age of the animal. Different parts of the same animal, will display a different color of meat. Muscles that are exercised frequently such as legs need more oxygen. *As a result they develop a darker color* unlike the breast which is white due to little exercise. This color is pretty much fixed and there is not much we can do about it unless we mix different meats together. Fat does not have myoglobin and curing it with *nitrite* will not change its white color.

Fish float in water and need less muscle energy to support their skeletons and that is why their meat is white, with some red meat around the fins, tail, and the more active parts of the fish which are used for swimming. As most of the fish don't have *myoglobin* the meat is not going to be pink and that explains why very few fish recipes include cure. The red color of some fish, such as salmon and trout, is due to astaxanthin, a naturally occurring pigment in the crustaceans they eat.

Chapter 2

Equipment

Equipment does not make sausages, you do. Regardless of how expensive or fancy the tool, it will not save your product if you grind warm meat, cook or smoke at too high temperatures. Don't start by buying an electric grinder or large capacity stuffer. Utilize kitchen equipment you already own, for example a food processor for making emulsified sausages. Proper equipment makes the job easier and faster which is important for making large amounts of product. Who cares how fast you grind meat or stuff the casing – what is important is the look and the taste of the finished product.

Cutting/Grinding
The manual grinder is a device that has been around for a long time. A grinder as the definition implies, grinds meat and pushes it through a plate, *it does not produce a perfectly clean cut*. There is a large amount of pressure on meat in the feed chamber. This leads to tearing between the auger and the walls of the chamber. As a result the meat is not cut as clean as with a sharp knife or a bowl cutter.

Photo 2.1 above, # 10 grinder.
Photo 2.2 # 10 grinder plates.
Photo 2.3 # 10 grinder knives.

What Grinder to Buy?

Although an electrical machine looks impressive, the question to ask is how much meat are we going to process? Manual grinders are *very efficient* machines and are very inexpensive. On the other hand, small home type electrical models cost more and work twice as fast at best. These are general estimates for the output capacity of different grinders:

Manual		Electric (Home Quality)	
Type	Capacity in lb per min.	Type	Capacity in lb per min.
# 10	2-3	# 10	5
# 22	3-4	# 22	9
# 32	4-5	# 32	12

The majority of recipes on the Internet ask for between two and five pounds of meat. This means that most people use less than one pork butt (around 6 lb) of meat. A number 10 grinder will do it in 3 minutes. If you plan making 50 pounds of sausage, yes, your hand will get tired and the electrical model is a logical choice, but check if it comes with different plates.

Bowl cutter - also known as buffalo chopper or silent cutter, can cut meat very finely and is a must have machine for commercial production of emulsified products such as bologna or hot dogs.

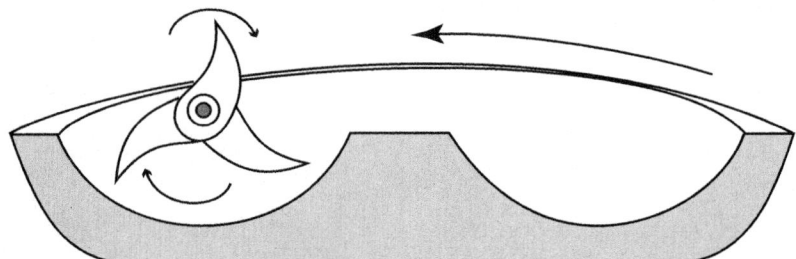

Fig 2.1 Operation of a bowl cutter.

Both the speed of the turning bowl and rotating knives are adjustable. The stainless steel bowl turns about 14-16 times per minute and the knives rotate about 3,000 times per minute. The resulting friction generates so much heat that the meat will boil and cook. To keep the temperature down crushed ice is added to the mixture. As the meat is finely comminuted, a lot of protein is released which in combination with salt and phosphates can easily absorb melting ice and the resulting water. The mixture becomes a fine paste which after stuffing becomes a hot dog, bologna or any emulsified sausage. The bowl cutter can be employed to make any kind of a sausage except fermented dry products. A negative aspect of bowl cutters is they are heavy and expensive.

Home Food Processors will take care of emulsifying sausages such as hot dogs, frankfurters, bologna and fine liver sausages. Commercial bowl cutters are overkill for home production.

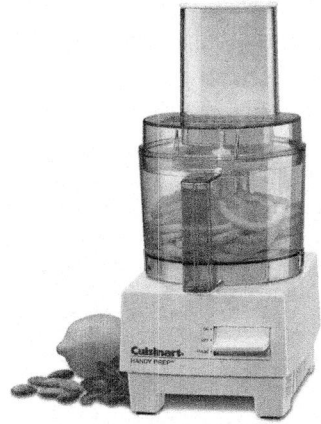

Photo 2.4 Cuisinart® Food Processor.

Stuffing Equipment

It is our opinion than a serious hobbyist should invest in a *vertical piston stuffer* which will make stuffing faster and more enjoyable. The money that is saved by not buying an electrically operated grinder can be reinvested into the purchase of a piston stuffer.

Vertical stuffers come from 5 lb to 25 lb capacity. Bigger units can be equipped with an electrical motor.

Photo 2.5 above, 15-lb capacity piston stuffer.

Sausages in the past were stuffed with fingers, a funnel, animal horn or any suitable device. Stuffing is a monotonous and labor intensive task and any tool will be of great help. The majority of hobbyists stuff sausages using grinders and the attached stuffing tube.

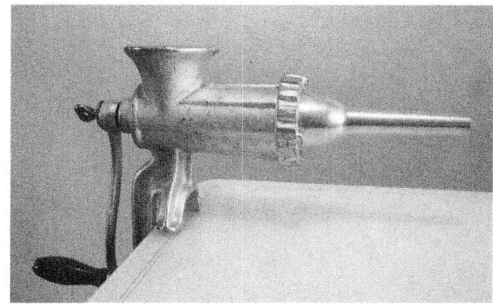

Photo 2.6 # 10 grinder with stuffing tube.

Weighing Scales

Digital scales are fine for weighing meats, however, get a small highly accurate scale for weighing spices. Such scale is a must have item for weighing starter culture when making fermented sausages since culture is added in microscopic amounts.

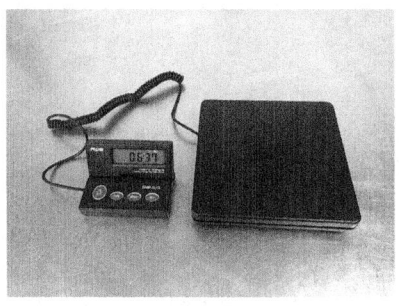

Photo 2.7 A typical kitchen scale made by Taylor.

Photo 2.8 A scale with a remote readout is convenient when weighing large containers. AWS-Ship-Elite, Model-SE-50

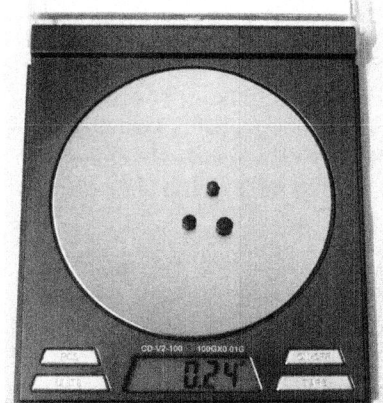

Photo 2.9 Weighing whole peppercorns on a very accurate AWS Compact Digital Scale v2.0 by *American Weigh Systems*
Capacity: 100 g
Accuracy: 0.01 g (0.001 oz)
Size: 5.6 x 4.9 x 0.5"

Thermometers

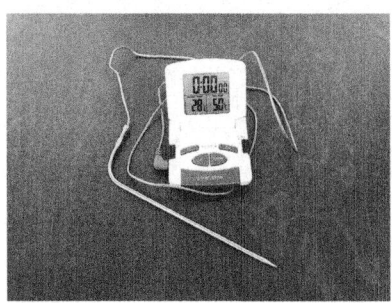

Photo 2.10 Needle thermometer is used to monitor meat's internal temperature.

Photo 2.11 Candy thermometer can be clipped to the side or hung on string.

Photo 2.12 These smoked butts were smoked to the perfect light brown color. They need to be cooked now until they reach the right temperature inside.

Photo 2.13 This is was accomplished with the candy thermometer monitoring water temperature and the needle temperature indicating the internal temperature of the butt.

Photo 2.14 The cooked butts were showered with cold water and air cooled.

Photo 2.15 This top quality product was made with the simplest equipment - it was pumped and immersed in curing solution, smoked, cooked, and cooled according to all established rules.

Cooking Pots

If you cook one or two sausages it does not really matter how tall a pot is, however, it is advisable to have a false bottom screen to prevent sausages from resting on the hot bottom. This may result in a burst casing and a mess in the pot. For cooking many sausages a taller pot is much better since you can transfer many sausages from the smokehouse in one movement. The smokestick rests on top of the pot and sausages are suspended in water well above the bottom. A second arrangement is to run twine around the sausages and slide the sausages off the stick to the pot, securing twine to the pot's handle.

Photo 2.16 Tall pot is needed for cooking many sausages.

It goes without saying that knives, cutting boards, spoons, strainers, butcher's twine, measuring cups and other kitchen items are needed as well.

Smokehouse

Think of a smokehouse as another tool, its purpose is to give meat a smoky flavor. It does not matter how expensive or fancy it is. It does not need to be perfectly tight, as long as the smoke makes contact with the meat, the product will acquire a smoky flavor. Any type of a structure will serve as a smokehouse: a wooden box, carboard box, steel drum, smokehouse made from loose concrete blocks, etc. The top can be loosely covered with plywood, burlap sack, steel plate as long as they allow us to adjust the amount of exiting smoke.

The design of a smokehouse becomes important when we intend to bake the sausages inside. Now we need to maintain a constant temperature of 60-85° C (140-185° F) to smoke meat inside and bake it. It is easier said than done. The structure must be tight now, more so if cooler temperatures are present. The smokehouse may need to have a gas or electric burner to provide a reliable and adjustable heat source. Maintaining constant temperature with burning wood is difficult at best, every time a fresh log is inserted the temperature drops, then the wood bursts into flames and the temperature is rapidly rising. It requires constant vigilance. Two thermometers are needed: one stem thermometer on the outside to displace the temperature inside of the smokehouse and another needle thermometer to monitor the internal temperature of the sausage. There is no difference between a "smoker" and a "smokehouse." On a farm meats were smoked and stored inside of a big walk-in shed. It had the roof, screened openings and a door, since the name: a "smokehouse".

You can buy a smoker or you can build it yourself.

Concrete Block Smoker

An excellent smoker can be built in no time by using standard 8" x 8" x 16" inexpensive concrete blocks. This is a totally flexible design and imagine that you are building a smoker like a child who is erecting a house using little building blocks. This is how this smoker is built and the only difference is that the blocks are slightly bigger: 8" x 8" x 16". The construction does not include using mortar, just arranging blocks in the manner that will be most practical. The required materials are available in a building supply store and the smoker can be built in a matter of hours.The easiest and fastest way to support the smokesticks is to place them directly on top of the smoker. The sticks should be 1" in diameter as they act as spacers now, separating the top of the smoker from the cardboard or wooden cover that rests on it. This creates ample space for the smoke to exit from the smoker.

Equipment for Making Fermented Sausages

Testing equipment such as Meat pH meter, pH testing strips or Aw water activity meter is recommended for persons involved in making fermented sausages and can be obtained on the internet. Fermenting and drying chambers can also be ordered but are very expensive, hower, they can be easily constructed at home.

To be able to precisely control temperature, humidity, and air speed requires expensive computer controlled drying chambers and a home sausage maker must use his ingenuity to come up with suitable solutions. Making fermented sausages at home definitely presents some difficulties, which we don't have to face when making other types of sausages. It is very helpful to have a system capable of automated temperature and humidity adjustments, but those with limited funds will need to improvise. Without a doubt the precise control of such a vast range of temperatures 10-40° C (50-104° F), and humidity (60-95%) is not easy.

Photo 2.17 Concrete block smoker. You can view more details about this and other designs at: www.meatsandsausages.com/smokehouse-plans/smokehouse-block

There are no small drying chambers designed for home production of fermented sausages, and one has to assemble his own system. Commercial producers use huge rooms with air conditioning ducts supplying air at the right temperature, humidity and speed. There is a refrigerator in every kitchen and that appliance can be quite easily adapted for fermenting and drying sausages. A used refrigerator can be obtained everywhere and as long as it works it will fit our purpose.

Temperature Control

There is a problem with the refrigerator's temperature range as its thermostat is made to control temperatures between 0-4° C (32-40° F). Such temperatures are not needed during fermenting and drying sausages. Fortunately, there is a commonly available device called a line voltage thermostat. It is an electronic temperature control or rather a combination of a temperature sensors, switches and electronic controls that can transform an ordinary refrigerator into a wonderful drying chamber. It is made by a few companies.

Line Voltage Thermostat - Single Stage

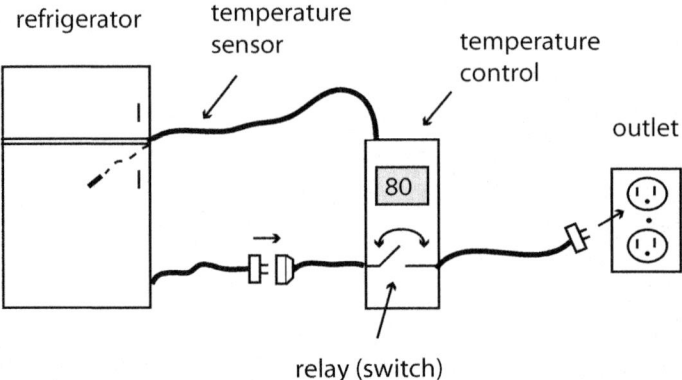

Fig. 2.2 Electronic temperature control in *cooler* mode.

A refrigerator is *unplugged* from the outlet and is then plugged into the temperature control which is plugged into the electrical outlet. The refrigerator's thermostat is not controlling the temperature anymore and is taken over by the temperature sensor in the controller, which is inserted into the refrigerator. There is no need to drill a hole as the refrigerator door has rubber insulation and the sensor's cable is thin. The microprocessor monitors the temperature through the sensor and when the temperature is warmer than the set point, the processor will energize the internal relay (switch). This allows the refrigerator to draw the current from the controller and start cooling. The drawing is not to scale and the typical unit is about: 6.5" x 2.7" x 2.5". These units can control coolers, heaters or any electrical devices.

The unit depicted in Fig. 2.2 is *a single stage control which means that it can control only one device at a time.* A line voltage thermostat set to "cooling mode" can only decrease temperature lower than the temperature that remains outside the refrigerator. There are instances when the temperature inside the chamber must be higher:

- Fast fermented sausages made with starter cultures which require fermentation temperatures of around 30-45° C (86 -113° F).
- Drying chamber is located in a cool climate where temperatures are below 20° C (68° F) for a larger part of the year. Under such circumstances the same line voltage thermostat can be combined with a heater and used in the heating mode.

In such a case the temperature control is switched to "heating mode", the refrigerator is *disconnected* and the heater is plugged into the temperature control. The refrigerator becomes just a drying chamber.

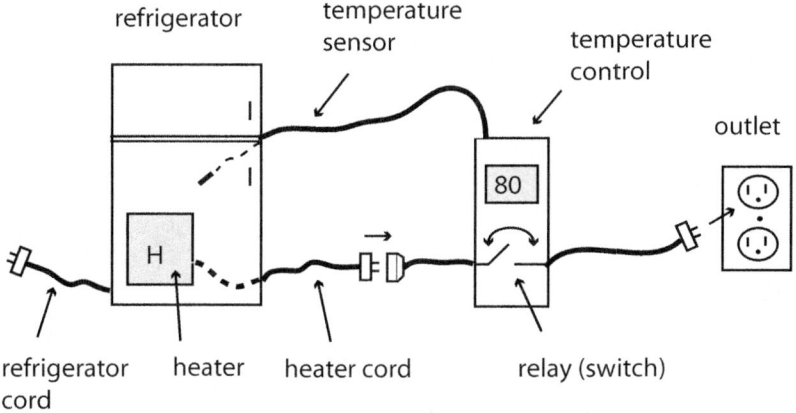

Fig. 2.3 Electronic temperature control in *heater* mode.

Any little heating element, ceramic heater, heat lamp or even a UL approved light fixture will easily raise the temperature in a small unit such as a refrigerator. Using an ordinary light bulb is not recommended as prolonged exposure to light creates rancidity in fat. Temperature control can be used in heating mode during fermentation, which lasts on average about 1-2 days and even less for fast fermented products. Then when a product enters the drying stage, the heater can be removed and the control unit is switched back into the cooling mode. When ambient temperatures are low and the heating mode is selected, the refrigerator can still be used as a drying chamber, even though it is disconnected from the power supply. In cooler climates it is practical to build a large drying chamber (even a walk in unit) from any materials, as long as the chamber is well insulated. Not being limited by space any kind of a free standing heater and humidifier can be placed inside providing there is electricity close by. These electronic temperature controls are very precise and can maintain the set temperature within 1 degree.

Line Voltage Thermostat - Two Stage

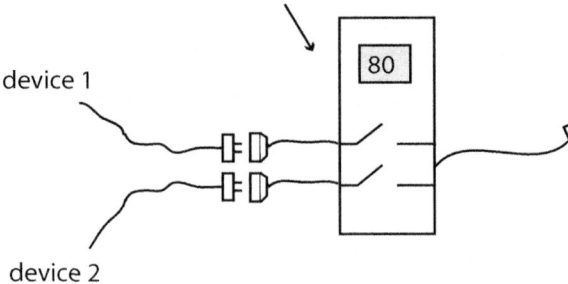

Fig. 2.4 Two stage line voltage thermostat.

The advantage of a two stage thermostat is that two independent devices such as a heater and a cooler, or a heater and fan can be connected to only one temperature control.

Humidity Control

Humidity control is much harder to accomplish than temperature. All those improvised arrangements such as placing salt covered with water in a shallow pan, or bringing more water filled pans into the chamber may increase the humidity level to 50-60%, which is nowhere close to the required humidity during fermentation.

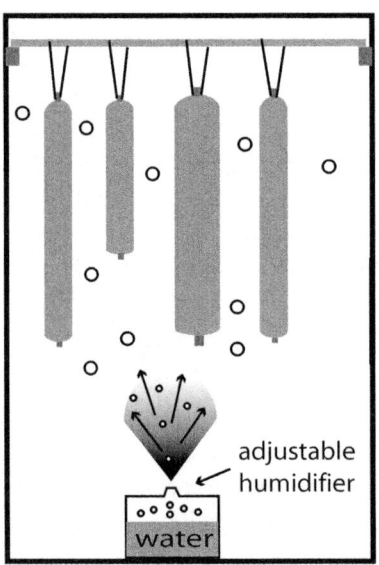

The simplest way to control humidity is to install a small digital adjustable humidifier. A good unit should lock to the setting within a few percents. In industrial units increasing humidity is accomplished by steam injection but home units produce a cool vapor mist.

It should be noted that an average hygrometer is rated to indicate humidity plus or minus 3% at best. In reality they are even less accurate (10%) but there are more expensive calibrated units that are accurate within 1%.

Fig. 2.5 Adjustable humidifier.

Air conditioners and refrigerators dehumidify air until the relative humidity is around 40%. This is much too low for making fermented sausages, especially at the beginning of the fermentation stage when 90-95% humidity is recommended. If a sausage is fermented without humidity control, periodic spraying or immersing it in water will help by providing 100% of humidity on its surface, if only for a short while.

There is a device called a line voltage humidistat which basically works like the temperature controls described earlier. When in "humidify" mode the device will increase humidity by switching on the humidifier. When in "dehumidify" mode the same device will switch on the fan to remove moist air from the chamber.

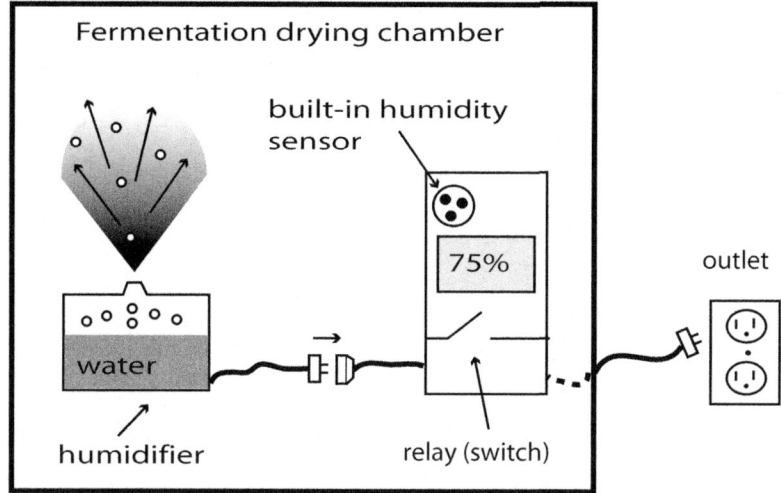

Fig. 2.6 Single stage humidistat.

The in-line voltage humidistat depicted above comes with a built-in humidity sensor and must be installed within the drying chamber. There is a humidistat which comes with a remote humidity sensor and a control unit can be mounted outside of the drying chamber. Humidity control plays an important role in greenhouse production of flowers and vegetables and many clever devices can be obtained from green house equipment suppliers.

Air Speed

Air speed is a factor that helps remove moisture and stale air, and of course it influences drying. Sausages will dry faster at higher temperatures, but in order to prevent the growth of bacteria, drying must be performed at lower levels, generally between 15-12° C (59-53° F). The speed of drying does not remain constant, but changes throughout the process: it is the fastest during the beginning of fermentation, then it slows down to a trickle. At the beginning of fermentation humidity is very high due to the high moisture content of the sausage. *When starter cultures are used, the temperature is at the highest during fermentation* which speeds up moisture escaping from the sausage.

The surface of the sausage contains a lot of moisture which must be constantly removed otherwise mold might appear. If the sausages are soaking wet during fermentation, the humidity should be lowered. At the beginning of fermentation the fastest air speed is applied, about 0.8 - 1.0 m/sec. *The speed of 3.6 km/h (2.2 mile/hour) corresponds to the speed of 1 meter/second.* Ideally, the amount of removed moisture should equal the amount of moisture moving to the surface.

To control air speed in improvised chambers such as a refrigerator is surprisingly easy. The most reliable device is a computer cooling fan as it is designed for working 24 hours a day. There is a huge variety of these fans and they come in different sizes, shapes and power outputs. They can be obtained online or at any computer store. The current draw of a typical 3" 12 VDC, 1.9 W fan is only 0.1 A. It runs from a 115 VAC adapter and the beauty of the design is that the adapter's output can be set to 12, 9, 7.5 or 6 VDC with a built in mini switch. Each voltage setting lets the fan run at a different speed and quite a sophisticated system is created.

If only a fixed DC output voltage adapter is available, a simple, inexpensive and universally available device called a "potentiometer" can be attached between the fan and the adapter. The device will control the fan's speed.

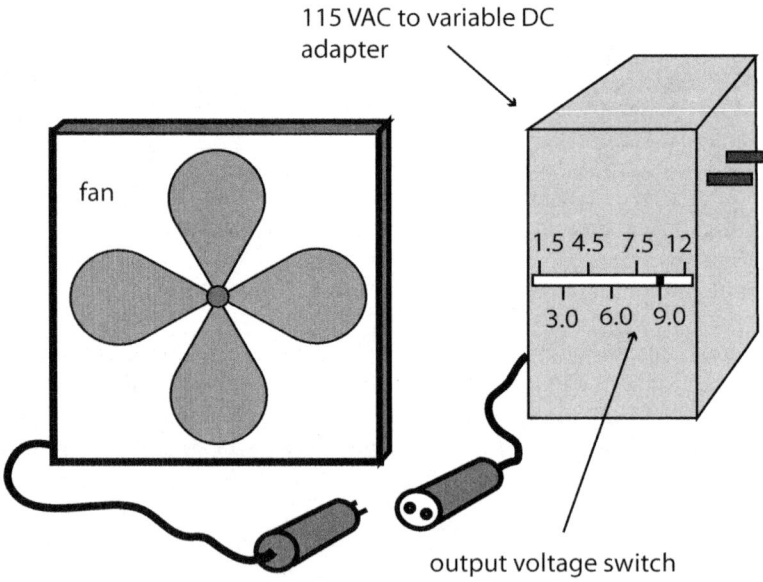

Fig. 2.7 Adjustable air speed fan.

Keep in mind that there must be an exhaust opening in the chamber for the removal of moisture, otherwise, the fan will continue to recirculate the same air which will become moister in time.

Chapter 3

Sausage Making Process

The sausage making process consists of the following steps:

- Meat selection. Meat may be cured before grinding
- Grinding
- Mixing
- Stuffing. Making fresh sausages ends with this step. Sausages may be smoked now (optional), they are often submitted to a short conditioning (drying) process (1-2 hours) before smoke is applied
- Cooking. Fermented/dry sausages are neither cooked nor cooled. Semi-dry fermented may be partially cooked
- Cooling
- Storing

Meat Selection

All cuts of good meat make good sausages. The trick is to know when and how to use them. Trim out all gristle, sinew, blood clots, and excess fat but save suitable trimmings for later. They can be used for making emulsified sausages or head cheeses. Those lower quality trimmings are hard to grind through a grinder but a food processor will chop them fine. If you choose only lean cuts, your sausage will definitely be healthier, but you will miss out on the taste. Most sausages are made of either pure pork, or a combination with other meats, most often beef. Sausages made entirely from beef will be drier with a harder texture.

Veal makes a light colored sausage and has excellent binding properties. Mutton can also be used in sausage. It has poor water holding properties and its distinctive flavor is not appreciated by many. For this reason it should be limited to around 15% in any recipe.

Sausages can be made from all kinds of meats, some of them quite exotic, but we limit our choices to meats that are common. Chicken is the most popular meat which is consumed worldwide as it is easy to raise and can be cooked and eaten by the average family at one sitting. Other meats of value are fish, venison and wild game. Sausages need about 25-30% of fat in them and when it comes to selecting meat for sausages, the majority of books and Internet recipes call for pork butt as it has the right lean meat to fat ratio of 70/30 and a beginner might think that only the butt can be used for making sausages.

Keep in mind that a pig has only two pork butts weighing together about 15 pounds but the farmer is left with an additional 250 pounds of meat that must be used. Without a doubt pork butt is a lovely cut for making sausages and the best choice for someone living in a large city as it is widely available and is economically priced. Its little blade bone is easy to remove and we are left with six pounds of lean meat, meat with some fat, meat with a lot of fat, some pure fat, connective tissue and the skin. When making sausages from pork butt, save the skin and fat for later use in a head cheese or liver sausage.

Picnic (front leg below butt) is a poor choice for a beginner but a great cut for someone who can make different types of sausages. It contains a lot of trimmings that can be used for making emulsified sausages, liver sausages and head cheeses. It requires much more work to trim it down into suitable pieces. In addition it contains a lot of connective tissue which will create hostile conditions for a regular home grinder. A bowl cuter or kitchen food processor is needed to effectively cut such trimmings.

Meat Classes

Imagine a butcher cutting pork into pieces until nothing is left on the table. Before he can carve out a ham from the leg he has to separate it from the body, then cut off the lower leg, remove the bones, tendons, gristle, sinews, skin, pieces of fat etc. To get a clean piece of meat like a ham, butt or pork loin a lot of work has to be performed first in order to separate scraps of meat that can not be sold in one piece.

Keep in mind that the meat plant was established to bring profits to its owners, and every little piece of meat, fat, and blood included is money. A commercial recipe does not call for pork butt, lean ham or beef chuck. The recipe asks for pork class 1, beef class 2 or back fat class 1 or 2. It may call for jowl or bacon fat. It really *does not matter whether this meat comes from ham, butt, picnic or from the container with little meat pieces* as long as it fulfills the requirements of the recipe. Only after all those scraps of meats are depleted, then a meat plant may resort to using noble parts such as ham or loin for sausages. All those trimmings end up in a cooler in labelled containers. Names such as ham, picnic or butt lose their meaning as one can only see cuts of meat with different fat contents. They have to be classified in some logical manner so they can be picked up from a cooler by any operator and transferred to production.

When meat is ground and placed for sale in a supermarket it is labeled as 85% lean, 70% lean or even 90% lean. When this meat is ground the calculations are made as to its fat content and more lean meat or more fat are added in order to comply with the requirement of a particular label. *It is a great idea to get into the habit of thinking in terms of meat classes or grades when making your own products.* Once we become familiar with this way of thinking we will be able to look at the cut of the meat and decide what will be the best product to use it for. All the time different meats are on sale and they can be bought at a good price and stored in a freezer until needed.

In a large meat plant cattle and pigs are slaughtered mainly into noble parts and the worker is faced with a problem of all those little scraps of meat, fats, sinews, gristle, skins, organs, head meat, etc. All those leftovers end up in bologna, hot dogs and frankfurters. People living on a farm have more control over the meat when the animal is slaughtered.

They can process still warm meat and thus obtain the highest quality product. It will be unrealistic to expect that the entire animal will be processed in a few hours, but at least meat cuts that are used for making special sausages such as head cheeses, and blood and liver sausages, should be processed as fast as possible and not later than the second day. Other cuts such as meat organs (liver, heart, lungs, kidneys) and blood must be frozen. It is more practical to throw split pork head and hocks into the kettle with boiling water and be over with it. Then meat can be processed on the same or on the following day. Blood keeps poorly so it makes sense to make blood sausages as soon as possible.

When carving ham or butt you will get all meat classes, of course in different proportions. Picnic which is mainly class III, will also provide class II or even a piece of meat class I. It is a good substitute for pork head meat. Let's assume that tripe is on sale. Well, there is nothing wrong with a tripe stew, ask anybody in Europe or any person of Spanish descent. Buy the tripe, precook it, grind it, add 20% into any sausage and your sausage will taste great, will cost you less and will have a lighter color. Tripe has poor binding qualities so you won't be able to add too much water.

Knowing meat classes will help you immensely when shopping for better deals at large supermarkets. You will understand what quality meat you will be buying, regardless what's on the label. Next time when trimming pork chops, loins or hams for roasting, save all those little meat pieces and put them into a freezer. You can use them to make sausages at a later date.

Fat

There are different types of fat and they all are used for different purposes. There are hard, medium and soft fats and they have a different texture and melting point.

Pork fat is preferred for making sausages as it is hard, white and tastes the best. It exhibits different degrees of hardness depending from which animal part it comes from. Back fat, jowl fat, or butt fat (surface area) have a very hard texture and higher melting point. These are the best choices for making products in which we expect to see the individual specks of fat in a finished product such as dry salami. Soft fat such as bacon fat is fine for making fermented spreadable sausages such as mettwurst or teewurst. For most sausages any fat pork trimmings are fine. providing they were partially frozen when submitted to the grinding process. If no back fat is available, use fat pork trimmings or meats which contain more fat and grind them together.

Beef fat has a higher melting temperature than pork but is yellowish in color which affects the appearance of the product where discrete particles of fat should be visible. Besides, beef fat does not taste as good as pork fat.

Chicken fat is neutral in flavor and is suited for making chicken sausages although it presents some problems. It is so soft and melts at such low temperatures that it is hard to work with.

Note: at room temperature every fat has a tendency to smear due to the temperature increase that results from the mechanical action of knives and the grinder's delivery worm. To overcome the problem of smearing fat should be processed partially frozen. Partially frozen back fat may be manually diced with ease into 1/8" (3 mm) pieces.

Grinding

The lean meat should be separated from the fat. As a rule, lean meat is ground coarsely while fatty cuts are ground very finely. This way our sausage is lean looking and the fat is less visible. It is much easier to grind cold meat taken directly out of the refrigerator. The question may arise, why do we grind different grades of meat through different plates? There are many reasons:

1. You could do just that if you had only high grade meats, let's say pork class I (ham) and pork class II (butt). With such fine meats you would not get any pieces of bone, gristle or sinews that would stick between your teeth. On the other hand, meat trimmings of lower classes would be hard to chew if they were not finely ground.

2. The second reason is that we want to retain meat juices and water inside the meat and those poor meat grades with a lot of gristle and sinews are loaded with collagen that help do just that. The cleaner grind we can obtain the stronger binding power meat develops and this is where a bowl cutter starts to shine. A grinder, manual or electrical, cuts meat and pushes meat through plate holes, cutting meat but also mechanically breaking it at the same time. A bowl cutter cuts cleanly without tearing the meat's structure. It generates a lot of heat so ice or cold water are added to cool down the meat and rotating knives.

That allows the meat to emulsify into the consistency of a fine paste that is able to trap all this ice and water and hold it inside. Chemicals like phosphates are very efficient at that. All scraps of meat with fat, gristle and sinews have become a paste now, the product will be juicier and the manufacturer will make more money by charging a customer for this trapped ice and water. This is exactly how we make low quality mass produced products such as hot dogs, frankfurters, bologna or liver sausages.

3. The third reason is that a lot of fat is being used to make sausages and it will be visible with the naked eye when we slice the sausage. By grinding fat through a fine plate the fat will bind with meat and will not be noticeable, a kind of cheating as we still eat the same amount of fat. There is not any rigid, fixed rule in regard to grinder plates and that the plate selection depends greatly on the type of sausage that you decide to make and the size of casing. For hundreds of years we chopped meat with knives and stuffed it with fingers through a horn. And the sausages were great.

Mixing

If the meat was previously cured, then salt and nitrite, were already added. Now we have to add the remaining spices. Use a big container to facilitate mixing. The lean meat should be mixed with spices first and the fat should be added at the last moment. Mixing meat by hand raises its temperature and should be done as quickly as possible. The time is important because fat specks start to melt at 95-104° F (35-40° C). We want to prevent this smearing to keep the sausage texture looking great. Spices may be premixed with cold water in a blender, and then poured over the minced meat. The water helps to evenly distribute the ingredients and it also helps soften the mass during stuffing. We can easily add 1 cup of cold water to 5 lbs. of meat because it is going to evaporate during smoking anyhow.

A rule of thumb is about 8% of water in relation to the weight of the meat. With most sausages it is customary to add some water to facilitate mixing. During cutting/ grinding meat proteins are released which is enhanced by adding salt. Those proteins dissolve readily in salt water and a sticky meat mass is obtained which results in a better binding and ultimately in better texture of the sausage. *Apply some force when mixing,* kneading might be a good word for it. *This will help to extract proteins* which will combine with salt and water and will create a sticky meat mass. This will hold meat particles together very well and will result in a good texture.

In fermented (dry) sausages the addition of water to the sausage mass should be cut down to a minimum, as this creates favorable conditions for the growth of bacteria and will prolong drying.

Stuffing

Taste the sausage before it's stuffed as there is sill time for last minute corrections. People make mistakes when reading recipes, they get confused with ounces and grams, they use different size spoons to measure ingredients, etc. Just make a very tiny hamburger, throw it on a frying pan and in two minutes you can taste your sausage. After the meat is mixed it has to be stuffed into a casing, preferably as soon as possible. Allowing the meat to sit overnight causes it to set up and absorb all this moisture that we have added during mixing and stuffing. The ample amount of salt inside will perform this trick and we'll be struggling with stuffing the casings the next day. This can be avoided by remixing the mixture. Although sausages should be stuffed as tightly as possible, nevertheless for practical reasons different sausage types are stuffed to a different degree of firmness.

The casing should have about a third of a cup of water inside as it acts as a lubricant for the entering meat. By the same token pouring water over the stuffing tube is recommended to increase lubrication. Some people grease the tube lightly. Don't use water when stuffing slow fermented sausages. Use the largest stuffing tube which fits the casing but make sure it goes on loosely otherwise the casing might break. It is important to stuff sausages hard and without air as the resulting air pockets might fill with water and become little holes later.

In fermented and dry products, such moisture pockets may become breeding grounds for bacteria. Natural and synthetic casings are used as long as they allow moisture and smoke to go through. They must be able to cling to meat and shrink with it as it goes through the drying process. Natural casings may look solid but in reality they contain minute pores that permit smoke or moisture to go through. Natural casings are salted and they must be prepared for stuffing:

- Soak casings in cold water for 30 minutes before use to eliminate salt and to make them pliable. Change water once or twice. To reduce any possibility of contamination by bacteria, rinse casings briefly (in and out) with vinegar. This is a good safety measure when making fermented sausages.

- If during drying the outside of the sausage becomes greasy, it should be wiped off with a warm cloth otherwise it may inhibit drying.

Casings

There is no substitute for natural casings. Pork casings will satisfy the majority of your needs, sheep casings are used for small diameter sausages like Vienna, Frankfurter or smoked Kabanosy. Pork bungs or beef casings are better for larger diameter casings or salami type sausages. The advantage of using natural casings is that they allow smoke penetration and moisture removal and they shrink with the sausage as it loses moisture (weight). Collagen are artificially produced natural casings which are easy to work with and allow smoke and moisture penetration. For sausages such as blood, liver and head cheese plastic casings are fine as there is no smoke or moisture movement. In some cases freshly cooked liver sausage is cooled and then briefly cold smoked for a longer shelf life and more unique flavor; in those instances use a natural casings. Natural casings when covered with salt will last in a refrigerator for years. Wash them and soak in water for 30 minutes before use.

Steps such as meat cutting, grinding, mixing and stuffing should be performed at temperatures below 12° C (54° F). When working at higher temperatures, try to plan and organize your work in such a way that the meats will be processed as fast as possible and then placed in a refrigerator. Whether a sausage is stuffed into 32, 36 or 38 mm hog casings, its taste will obviously remain the same, however, the smoking and cooking times will change accordingly. The casing is just a packing material and although some traditionally made products may look unusual if stuffed into plastic casings, they will taste the same.

Conditioning

This is the drying/setting step which at the first look seems to be insignificant but in reality it is very important as stuffed sausages may contain meat that was only partially cured. Leaving sausages for 12 hours at 2-6°C (35-42°F) or for 1-2 hours at room temperature will provide extra time to fully cure the meat.

Photo 3.1 Stuffed sausages waiting for smoking. This drying process is often performed inside the smoker and lasts about 1 hr (no smoke applied) at 40-54°C (104-130°F) until the casings feel dry. The time depends on the diameter of the sausage and the amount of moisture it contains.

This simple process dries out the surface of the casing so it can develop proper smoking color. Conditioning may be performed in a smoker (no smoke applied) until the casings are dry. Leave draft controls or the top of your smoker fully open to let the moisture out. If natural wood is used for fuel, enough wood must be burned to produce sufficient amounts of hot embers that would be releasing heat without creating smoke to dry out the casings. Preheating a smoker to eliminate the humidity inside is a must step for the smoking process that follows.

Smoking Meats

Nothing improves flavor of meat or fish as smoking. Smoking meats is a favored topic on any meat forum, however, there are different interpretations of smoking methods and temperatures.

Mystery of Cold Smoking

Let us first correct a flawed and universally repeated theory that smoking preserves meat. It is technically not true; however, the theory dates back to times when we lived in primitive caves. Since we don't live in caves anymore it is time to correct it.

A big discovery was once made when someone by chance placed meat next to a fire. The meat developed a nice flavor and did not spoil so rapidly. The longer it stayed by the fire the longer it kept without spoiling. There is no way to deny this fact, it is as true today as it was thousands of years ago.

The big difference is that *not smoke but the warm drying air* preserved the meat. The warm air forced the moisture to escape from the meat and the product became more stable, because as we all know today bacteria cannot live when the moisture is taken away from them. Since the warm air was produced by burning wood and that always produces smoke, it was assumed that smoke was preserving the meat.

The correct definition is that the meat was *"drying with smoke"* – it was dried with air and *smoke just happened to be there.* Smoke is not needed to dry meat – sliced meat will dry in a dehydrator within a few hours without any smoke.

The majority of professional books in European countries where cold smoking is popular such as Poland or Germany recommend cold smoking temperature at 18-25° C (64-77° F). At this temperature the surface of the casings remains soft and the smoke and warm air can travel freely through the pores of the casing. The smoke creates the flavor, the air warms up the moisture inside escape through the casings to the outside. A sausage dries from inside out.

Smoking Methods

Cold smoking - 18-25° C (64-77° F), though it may be lower than 18° C (64 °F).

Warm smoking - is the first stage of hot smoking. Anything above cold smoking (25°C/77°F) and below hot smoking (40°C/104°F) fits this description. Meats and sausages are usually not smoked at warm smoking temperatures. This is where foods enter the "danger zone" (40-60° C/104-140° F), the temperature which facilitate growth of bacteria.

Hot smoking - above warm smoking, usually performed at 60° C (140° F) as this temperature gives us a good texture and smooth surface. Going higher will make sausages shriveled on outside and will melt the fat inside. Some sausages are smoked/baked even at 85° C (185° F) for shorter times, but they are an exception.

It is difficult to pinpoint the dividing line between different smoking methods. *The dividing line which separates cold smoking is the temperature when meat or fish proteins start to cook or using the technical term "coagulate."*

Coagulation is defined as the transformation of proteins from a liquid state to a solid form. Throw an egg on a cold frying pan and start raising the heat. At a certain point the white of the egg which actually looks like a clear jelly starts to coagulate (cook). The coagulation process starts in the egg white at a temperature of 57° C (134° F), however, for the egg yolk a higher temperature of around 65° C (149° F) is required.

In meat myosin protein begins to denature (unwind, lose structure) around 40° C (104° F) there is a rapid loss of moisture and the texture of the meat becomes harder. This will inhibit smoke penetration and the removal of moisture. These temperatures belong to the hot smoking method.

Smoking Sausages Without Nitrite

A common question is: can I smoke meats without nitrite? Of course you can. As explained earlier, you have to smoke your sausage at above 77° C (170° F) to get out of the "danger zone" which will affect its texture and make it greasy on the outside. Meat will lose its desirable red color. You may like it, but a commercial plant cannot produce products which might be ignored by the consumer. And they will be under scrutiny and constant supervision of meat inspectors to prevent any safety issues that might arise. In plain words smoking without nitrite is looking for trouble.

The Length of Smoking

This criteria is very loosely defined. Smoking today is just a flavoring step which is stopped *when the desired color is obtained.* Preservation is accomplished by *cooking* and keeping the product in a refrigerator. In the past cold smoking/drying continued for weeks so it was the preservation method. Hot smoking is performed with dense smoke and smoke deposition is more intense at higher temperatures. About one hour of hot smoking time for 1" (25 mm) of sausage diameter is plenty. If your sausage is stuffed into 36 mm casing 1½ hours is fine. If it is smoked for 2 or 3 hours, the smoky flavor will be more intense. Smoking much longer with heavy smoke might create a bitter flavor.

The stuffed sausages must feel dry, eventually slightly tacky to touch before smoke is applied.

Wood for Smoking

Any hardwood is fine but soft evergreen trees like fir, spruce, pine, or others cause problems. They contain too much resin and the finished product had a turpentine flavor to it, although in Germany and France certain sausages are smoked with such wood. Some popular woods:

- Alder – light flavor that works well with fish and poultry. Contains a hint of sweetness, good with poultry and wild fowl. Traditionally used for smoking salmon in Pacific Northwest. Popular in Poland.
- Beech - very good. Popular in Germany, Poland, Russia and other countries.

- Oak – probably best all around wood for meat smoking. Strong but not overpowering, good for sausages, beef or lamb. Smoked products develop a light brown to brown color, depending on the length of smoking. Popular in England and worldwide.
- Hickory – strong flavor, good with beef and lamb. Smoked products develop a reddish color. Grows in southern regions of the USA.

The color of the sausage can be influenced by wood: oak-brown color, hickory-reddish color. Mixing oak with hickory would create in-between red-brown color. All fruit and nut trees are suitable for smoking. The fact remains that wood from locally grown trees is used for smoking. If alder, oak or beech grow in the area people are not going to order cherry or pecan wood.

Wet wood is not for cold smoking because the purpose of cold smoking is to eliminate moisture, not bring it in. D*ry wood* is used for smoking slow-fermented dry sausages. Wet chips or sawdust seem to produce more smoke but this is hardly true. The extra amount of smoke is nothing else but water vapor (steam) mixed with smoke. This, however, does make a difference when hot smoking at 105-140° F, (40-60° C) and the smoke times are short. That extra moisture prevents the sausage casings from drying out during smoking, however, wet chips are not going to be wet for very long; the heat will dry them out anyhow.

In the past sausages were smoked for different reasons. Our ancestors did not care much about the flavor of the meat or the sausage. What they needed was a method that would preserve food for later. They tried different methods to preserve meat and this eventually lead to salt curing, drying, smoking and fermenting. It was discovered that salted meats could be air dried and would keep for a long time. Soon two different methods of drying developed.

In Northern Europe winters were cold and the only way meat could be dried was by placing it close to a fire. Originally that took place in caves where fire was the center of all social activities, then separate enclosures (smokehouses) were built for drying and storing meats. People became accustomed to smoke and smoking meats became popular.

In Southern Europe the moderate climate was less humid, the slightly blowing winds were ever present and meats were easily dried in the open air for most of the year. Since there was no need need to burn fires, Spanish chorizo and Italian salami were made by drying and meat smoking has never become popular as in the North.

Wood Pieces, Wood Chips or Sawdust

The type of wood used will largely depend on the smoker used and the location of the fire pit. If the smoker is connected with a fire pit by a pipe or a trench, it makes absolutely no difference what type of wood is burned as this a very practical design which provides efficient and comfortable smoke generation. Most people that use these types of smokers don't even bother with chips or sawdust and burn solid wood logs instead.

The type of wood used will largely depend on the smoker used, and the location of the fire pit. If the smoker is connected with a fire pit by a pipe or a trench, it makes absolutely no difference what type of wood is burned as this design can take a lot of abuse and still provides efficient and comfortable smoke generation. Most people that use these types of smokers don't even bother with chips or sawdust and burn solid wood logs instead.

Burning wood inside of small one-unit smokers creates the danger of a fire erupting. A safety baffle is installed to prevent flames from reaching upwards. This also prevents fat from dripping down on the wood chips and starting a big fire. When preparing sawdust, do not throw it into water, but place it in a bucket and then moisten it using a spray bottle. Mix sawdust by hand until it feels moist. Such sawdust burns longer and at lower temperatures than other woods. It is a preferred fuel for small electrical smokers sold by department stores.

When smoking in a home smoker with a fire pit in the bottom part of the drum, it is much easier to control the smoking process by using dry chips. These smolder and burn in a more predictable manner. Wet chips are moist on the outside only. even when placed in a bucket overnight.

Notes

- Touch your sausages during smoking, if they feel greasy the temperature is too high.
- The internal temperature of the meat or a sausage lags the temperature of the smoking/cooking chamber by about 15-25 degrees, depending on the thickness of the product.
- The temperature inside the sausage is lower than near the surface, depending on diameter. Once the heat is turned off, the internal temperature of the sausage will still increase by 1 or 2 degrees.
- Learn how to estimate temperature inside by grabbing the wooden smokestick which holds the sausages. Just check your feel with a thermometer and in time you will be able to estimate the temperature.
- If the outside temperature is over 25° C (77° F) you cannot produce cold smoke as the smoke will pick up some heat from burning wood or sawdust. Try to smoke at night when the temperature drops.
- Cold smoking is not a continuous process, you can smoke at night then hold sausages in a cooler during the day. Then repeat the process as many times as needed.
- Hot smoking is not barbecuing or grilling, it is performed at much lower temperatures.
- A hot, dense smoke delivers flavor faster than a cold thin smoke. Hot smoking will not preserve meat, however, it will provide some protection against bacteria in the surface area. When the smoking stops bacteria will try to invade the sausage again. However, a 28 mm diameter smoked sausage, made with 2% salt and sodium nitrite will lose moisture when placed in a refrigerator and will not spoil as it will become a dry sausage.

Cooking Sausages

All sausages must be cooked before serving except salami type dry sausages and fermented spreadable sausages such as German Mettwurst, Teewurst, Spanish Sobrasada or Polish Metka. The sausage making process can finish with the stuffing step, but the sausage must must be refrigerated and cooked before serving or be frozen for later use. In most cases a stuffed sausage is immediately cooked, although it may be smoked first.

People who win barbecuing contests always follow the golden rule: "cook low and cook it slow." and the same rule applies to sausage making with one notable difference - the smoking and cooking temperatures are even lower.

Fats start to melt at 35-40° C (95-104° F) and going over 76° C (170° F) internal meat temperature will decrease the quality of the sausage. Staying within 68-72° C (154-160° F) will produce the highest quality product. Special sausages such as blood sausage, liver sausage and head cheese have their ingredients pre-cooked before being minced, mixed and stuffed. As different cuts like skins, tongues, or jowls for example, will call for different cooking times it may seem that many pots might be needed. The solution is to use one pot but place the meats in separate bags made of netting. Each bag is removed as soon as the meat in it is cooked sufficiently.

Photo 3.2
Placing cuts in a bag facilitates their removal from hot water.

The leftover stock should be saved and used as a cooking medium for cooking sausages. If not enough stock remains, add more water. After sausages are cooked the remaining stock may be used for a soup.

Cooking in Water

People seldom realize that most sausages, including smoked ones, are cooked in hot water, which on average takes 15-60 minutes, depending on the diameter of the product. This method is easier and faster than baking in a smoker and the meat weight loss is smaller. This is due to the fact that *water conducts heat more efficiently than air*. Cooking in water is an acceptable and professional way of cooking sausages. There are dozens of known products that are made this way: regular smoked sausages, liver and blood sausages, head cheeses, butts and hams. Water is brought to the temperature of 70-90° C (158-194° F) and the meats or sausages are immersed in it.

For instance, home made hams are poached at 80° C (176° F) and this temperature is maintained until the meat's inside temperature reaches 69° C (156° F). Some recipes call for preheating the water before adding the sausages and some call for adding the sausages to cold water. Most people prefer the latter method. The poaching water should be heated rapidly to 80-85° C (175-185° F). A product taken out of the hot vessel might still increase its internal temperature by one or two degrees. A cooking pot remains uncovered during water cooking.

The poaching method is the preferred choice for sausages that are smoked with hot smoke. The short hot smoking process creates a dry layer on the outside of the sausage, similar to a second skin, that prevents the migration of moisture and juices from inside of the sausage to the water. Exact times and temperatures of poaching are given with particular recipes. At 80° C (176° F) the sausages are poached from 10-120 minutes, depending on the type and size of the product. A rule of thumb calls for about 30 minutes per pound, depending, of course on the cooking temperature. Some recipes call for preheating the water before adding the sausages and some call for adding the sausages to cold water. Most people prefer the latter method. It is generally accepted that 10 minutes are needed for each 1 cm of the width (diameter) of the sausage.

Poaching times for products up to 60 mm in diameter:

- Typical sausage - 10 min per 1 cm. Sausage 30 mm diameter is cooked 30 minutes.
- Liver sausage - 12 min per 1 cm. Sausage 50 mm in diameter is cooked 60 minutes.
- Blood sausage - 15 min per 1 cm. Sausage 40 mm in diameter is cooked 60 minutes.

Once the diameter of the sausage is larger than 60 mm, the above times are less accurate and should be increased. Double up the time, it is better to be safe than sorry. For example pork stomach may be cooked for 2-3 hours. *The best solution is to use a meat thermometer.*

Photo 3.3
Cooking ham and sausages in the same pot. The ham, will of course cook much longer.

Photo 3.4
Tying sausages into bundles helps to move them in and out of the hot water. The string is usually tied up to the pot's handle.

Baking in a Smoker

It seems like baking sausages in a smokehouse is a good idea as they are already there, however, cooking in water is more efficient as the air conducts heat poorly. On the other hand baked sausages look better having a glossy appearance on the outside. This is due to the fat that has melted under the surface of the casing and moved to the surface where it resides as a thin coat of grease. It is like putting grease on a pair of boots, they are going to shine and look better. Besides the looks the flavor of a baked sausage is also slightly better as there was no loss of meat juices which in the case of poached sausages will migrate to the water. The disadvantage is that the baked sausage loses more weight than the same sausage poached in water. Baking in a smoker is the slowest and the most difficult method that largely depends on the technical possibilities of the smoker.

While it takes 1-2 hours to smoke a sausage, it may take an additional 3 hours to cook it inside the smoker. It will largely depend on the inside temperature of the meat when smoking was stopped and the diameter of the sausage. If it was 38° C (100° F) we have a long way to go, if it was (66° C (150° F) we are almost there. That shows a need for some intelligent planning and it is advisable to slowly *increase the smoking temperature* to about 160° F. When smoking is done, the temperature should be increased to 77° C (170° F) and maintained at that level until the inside temperature of the smoked meat reaches 69° C (155° F). The product is both smoked and cooked. A lot will depend on *outside conditions and how well the smoker is insulated.* That may be difficult to achieve and we will have to increase the temperature of a smoker to about 85° C (185° F) to bring the internal temperature of the meat to the required level.

The other easier method is to set the temperature of the smoker to 77-80° C (170-176° F) and wait until the meat's inside temperature reaches 68° C (154° F). Choosing the cooking method is basically up to you, the dividing line may be the diameter of the sausage and the technical possibilities of your smoker.

Note: commercial producers use steam cooking. A rapid method but needs expensive equipment.

Cooling Sausages

Immediately after cooking the sausages should be showered with cold water. This procedure prevents shriveling of the sausages and removes some of the grease. Cooling sausages with water offers the following advantages:

• Cleans the surface from grease.

• Extends the product's shelf life.

• Decreases the time of air cooling which subsequently follows.

Photo 3.5 Sausages being cooled.

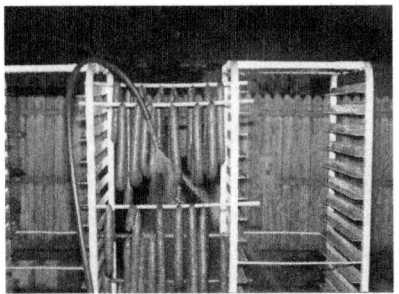

Photo 3.6 Smoked sausages showered with water.

Sausages should remain at temperatures between 55 - 10° C (130-50° F) for the shortest time possible as this temperature range facilitates the growth of bacteria. Although bacteria have been killed during the cooking process, new bacteria is anxious to jump back into the sausages surface. Cooling time depends on the diameter of the product but it may be estimated as:

- Small diameter sausages such as frankfurters - 5-10 min.
- Large diameter sausages - 15-20 minutes.

During this cooling/drying process a smoked sausage will further improve its shine, color, and will develop a darker shade of brown. Sausages should be hung in a dark place with a newspaper on the floor to catch any grease dripping down. After that the sausage can be refrigerated. The official recommendation of the Food Safety and Inspection Service of the USDA (June 1999) issues the following guidelines:

"During cooling, the product's maximum internal temperature should not remain between 130° F (54° C) and 80° F (27° C) for more than 1.5 hours nor between 80° F (27° C) and 40° F (4° C) for more than 5 hours" (6.5 hours total time). "Products cured with a minimum of 100 ppm ingoing sodium nitrite may be cooled so that the maximum internal temperature is reduced from 130° F (55° C) to 80° F (27° C) in 5 hours and from 80° F (27° C) to 45° F (7° C) in 10 hours" (15 hours total time).

Storing Meat

All uncooked sausages should be stored in a refrigerator or freezer. Cooked sausages should not be stored for more than 7 days if held at 5° C (41° F), or 4 days at 7° C (45° F). This practice will help control the growth of *Listeria monocytogenes*, a harmful bacteria. Meat products stored in a freezer for more than 3 months will start developing an inferior taste due to the oxidation of fat. Those chemical changes known as "rancidity" occur spontaneously and are triggered by light or oxygen. Meats stored in a freezer will turn rancid at a slower rate than meats stored in a refrigerator. Rancidity is not noticeable when meat is stored in refrigerator because it is consumed well before rancidity begins. To prevent fat oxidation and to prolong shelf-life of the product, antioxidants such as BHA, BHT, TBHQ and rosemary extracts are commonly used.

Chapter 4

Making Different Types of Sausages

Fresh Sausages

A fresh sausage is the simplest sausage of all. It is is neither cooked nor smoked and that explains the ease of its production. It is basically spiced hamburger meat stuffed into a casing. Fresh sausage is meant to be consumed on the same day, it may be kept for a few days in a refrigerator or may be frozen for later. In all cases the sausage must be fully cooked before serving.

The taste of the sausage will depend on meats that were selected and spices which were added to the mix. If you want to make Italian sausage use fennel which is the dominant spice in the recipe. To create a medium hot or hot version of the sausage add more or less of red pepper or cayenne. Providing that fresh meat is obtained and safety practices are implemented there is little to worry about *Salmonella*, *E.coli* or *Clostridium botulinum* as high heat during cooking takes care of those pathogens. Fresh sausages are stuffed into natural edible casings.

Fresh sausages contain much fat which is shown in the table that follows. The data comes from U.S. CFR 319. 140.

Name	Max Fat in %	Max Water in %
Fresh Pork Sausage	50	3
Fresh Beef Sausage	30	3
Breakfast Sausage	50	3
Italian Sausage	35	3

Due to their high fat content they taste delicious when fried or cooked on a grill.

Cooked Sausages

Cooked sausage is sausage that has been submitted to a thermal process. If the meat reaches $72°$ C ($160°$ F) inside temperature the sausage is fully cooked and can be eaten at any time. Its shelf life is longer than that of a fresh sausage because the heating process killed all bacteria, however, a new bacteria will invade the sausage in time again. For that reason, it should be kept in a refrigerator or frozen for later. Cooked sausages can be consumed cold but they taste better when served hot.

Smoked/Cooked Sausages

Many cooked sausages are flavored with smoke first. Smoking, regardless whether cold or hot, does not make a sausage safe, so after smoking the sausage is fully cooked. Sodium nitrite is added to minced meat to eliminate the danger of food poisoning, They must be be stuffed into *permeable* casings - the casings that allow smoke and moisture to go through. Natural and collagen casings are edible permeable casings. There are hundreds of cooked sausages, some made with meat only, others in addition to meat include materials such as groats, oats, rice, potatoes, bread, flour and more. Cooked sausages such as emulsified, liver, blood and head cheese are processed differently and are discussed in the pages that follow.

Emulsified Sausages

Emulsified sausages are *cooked* sausages that have been finely comminuted to the consistency of a fine paste. Hot dog, frankfurter, mortadella, bologna, liver sausage, pâté are typical examples. In most cases they are smoked and cooked with moist heat (steamed or in hot water). The first emulsified sausage was probably the German frankfurter, followed by the Austrian wiener. In the 1800's German immigrants brought these recipes to America and originally these sausages were served like any other.

Emulsified sausages can be divided in two groups:

1. High quality products made at home such as Austrian wiener or Polish Serdelki which are made from high quality meats and *without chemicals.* Beef, veal and pork are the meats commonly used. Beef frankfurter contains beef only. High quality products, for example frankfurter made with 40-60% lean beef, contain enough lean meat to absorb the necessary water without help from water retention agents.

2. Low quality commercial products are made from all types of meat trimmings (pork, beef, chicken, turkey), including machine separated meat. Chicken hot dogs, turkey hot dogs and all possible combinations can be found in a supermarket. *A large number of chemicals, water binding agents, fats and water are added* during manufacturing to compensate for lower meat grades.

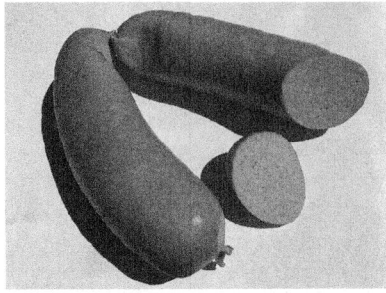

Photo 4.1 Emulsified Polish "Serdelki" sausage.

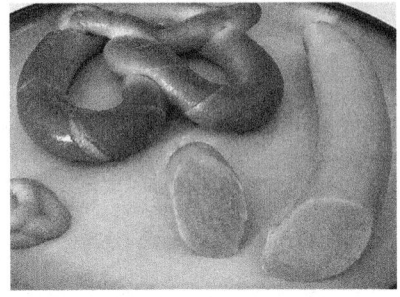

Photo 4.2 Emulsified German "Bratwurst" sausage.

Emulsification will be successful if the following criteria are met:

- Enough lean meat has been selected. The lean meat is the main source of *myosin*. The more myosin extracted, the thicker and stronger protein coat develops around particles of fat.

- Enough *myosin* has been extracted. This depends on how vigorous the cutting process was and how much salt (and phosphates) was added.

Too much fat especially when finely comminuted, will create such a large surface area that *there will not be enough protein solution to coat all fat particles*. As a result pockets of fat will form inside of the sausage. Some moisture is lost during smoking, cooking, and storing, and this factor must be allowed for in the manufacturing process. To make up for those losses more water is added during chopping/emulsifying. Experienced sausage makers know that the meats used in the manufacturing of sausages exhibit different abilities at holding water. Lean meat can hold more water than fatty tissue. Organ meats such as heart, glands, pork and beef tripe, pork skin, or snout all have *poor* water holding capabilities. Red meat found in pork head exhibits good water holding capability. Generally speaking any lean red meat holds water well although beef is on top of the list.

- Beef – high
- Veal – medium
- Pork – medium

Beef meat can absorb significant amounts of water:

- Bull meat – up to 100%
- Shank meat – up to 70%
- Cow meat – up to 60%
- Cheek meat – up to 40%

In simple terms 100 lbs of cow meat can absorb 60 lb of water and 100 lb of bull meat can absorb 100 lbs of water. An average beef piece bought in a local supermarket should hold about 30-40% of added water. To make top quality emulsified sausages at home a combination of lean red muscle meats should be used. This does not mean that only best lean cuts of meat must be employed.

Using meat trimmings is in fact encouraged. A typical frankfurter recipe consists of about 60% beef and 40% pork trimmings. Those trimmings may consist of cheaper grades of meat such as heart, cheek meat, pork or beef tripe, and fats. As long as lean beef is used to bind water, other "filler" meats may be added.

A commercial manufacturer can not afford the luxury of using only top quality meats so to keep the costs down he has to use second grade meat trimmings. Keep in mind that there is nothing wrong with such meats from a nutritional point of view, but in order to successfully incorporate them in a sausage we have to resort to water binding agents which will help to absorb and hold water within the meat structure.

If you study original instructions for making emulsified sausages from earlier times when chemicals were not yet widely used, you will see that beef was always ground with a smaller plate than pork. This was done in order to fully extract meat proteins which allowed meat to absorb more water. As finer meat particles are obtained, more protein is extracted and more water can be absorbed by the meat.

The fats are not going to hold water and it makes little sense to emulsify them as fine as lean meat. If show meats (larger pieces) or chunks of fat (Mortadella) are required, they will be mixed with an emulsified sausage mass in a mixer.

Water

Water plays an important part:

- It helps to extract water soluble proteins (*actin* and myosin) which contribute to better meat binding and strong emulsion.
- It helps to keep temperature down by adding ice to the bowl cutter.

Manufacturing Process

Meat selection. Lean beef, veal, lean pork. Keep in mind that the color of the sausage will depend on the type of meat used (*myoglobin* content) and to a smaller degree on spices.

Fat. About 20% of fat is needed for good texture, taste and flavor. Hard and soft fats can be used. Pork fat, beef fat, mutton fat, chicken fat or even vegetable oils can be utilized. Beef and lamb fat have a very strong flavor which can be masked by a careful selection of spices.

Examples of typical low cost meat formulas:

Formula A. Beef trimmings 60% (80% lean, 20% fat),
Pork trimmings 40% (80% lean, 20% fat).

Formula B. Beef trimmings - 50% (80% lean, 20% fat),
Pork trimmings - 50% (80% lean, 20% fat).

Curing meat. To obtain the highest quality sausage the meat should be properly cured with salt and sodium nitrite (Cure #1).This will produce a pink color typical to frankfurters or bologna. The smaller meat particle size requires a shorter curing time and emulsified meats are often cured using the faster "alternative curing" method. Salt and sodium nitrite are mixed with all ingredients and the stuffed sausage is allowed to rest for 1-2 hours. Then it will be smoked and cooked.

Grinding/Emulsifying. To lower costs a commercial producer will perform the first stages of production entirely in a bowl cutter. This saves time and space, simplifies equipment and allows the introduction of huge amounts of water. This is possible due to the addition of sodium erythorbate or ascorbic acid, which accelerates the production of nitric oxide (NO) from sodium nitrite (Cure #1). Nitric oxide reacts with meat myoglobin rapidly producing nitrosomyoglobin (NOMb). As a result the cured red color is obtained much faster and is more stable.

A typical emulsifying process

1. Add beef to a bowl cutter rotating on low speed.
2. Add salt, sodium nitrite (Cure#1), phosphates (if used) and 1/3 of finely crushed ice. Cut on high speed.
3. Add lean pork trimmings and another 1/3 of ice.
4. Add last part of ice, all spices, color enhancers (ascorbic acid, sodium erythorbate etc), fat and fat pork trimmings. Cut and mix together.

- Fat is added last as it does not absorb water and smears easily.
- Ascorbic acid reacts sporadically when in direct contact with sodium nitrite. This is why sodium nitrite is added at the beginning and ascorbic acid last.
- About 2-3% salt and 0.3-0.5% phosphates is added for maximum protein extraction.
- Salt soluble proteins are most effectively extracted from lean meat at 36-38° F (2-4° C).

Home Production

Grinding. Grind all meats with a coarse plate 3/8" (10 mm), refreeze and grind again through 3/16" (5 mm) or 1/8" (3 mm). Refreeze the mixture briefly and grind the third time through 1/8" (3 mm) plate. Continue adding a little amount of cold water when grinding to enhance the extraction of proteins.

Using Food Processor

A food processor allows to effectively chop meat trimmings that contain a lot of connective tissue, the task which will be hard to perform with a manual grinder. The meat should be first ground in a grinder through 1/8" (3 mm) plate and then emulsified in a food processor. Add a little amount of cold water or flaked ice to enhance extraction of proteins and to lower the meat's temperature resulting from the cutting blade's action.

Different meats can absorb different amounts of water, but adding 25% of crushed ice may be a good estimate. This will result in 10% sausage yield. Chop meat and fat adding crushed ice until it is completely absorbed. Meat should be emulsified until its temperature reaches 57° F (14° C). Above 60° F (15° C), the emulsion will be lost and the fat will separate from water and meat. In a properly emulsified meat there should be no distinction between meat and fat particles. You may add all ingredients into the food processor which will eliminate the mixing process.

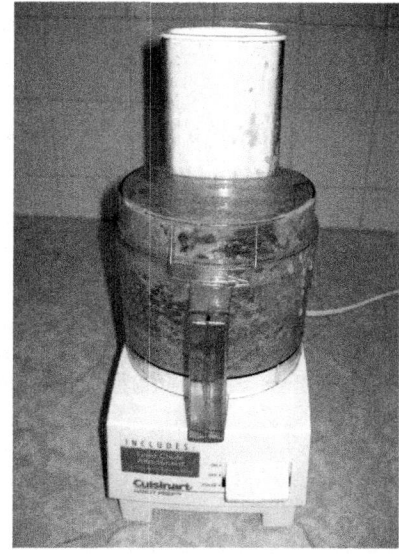

Photo 4.3 Cuisinart® food processors can chop and emulsify a variety of foods, including meat.

Note: adding some non-fat dry milk (3%), although not necessary, will strength the emulsion and will help the finished sausage retain moisture.

Photo 4.4 Commercial bowl cutter.

Emulsion breakdown occurs at 18° C (64° F) and obviously this temperature should not be crossed. A big advantage of using a bowl cutter is that mixing becomes a part of the process.

Basic processing steps during bowl cutting:

- Cut lean meat.
- Add seasonings and ice.
- Add extenders and binders (starch, rusk).

A large amount of meat proteins (mainly *myosin*) are extracted during cutting. They combine with salt and form a protein solution (exudate). *Myosin* is the protein most instrumental for making emulsion, *actin* exhibits preference for binding water. This solution provides the following benefits:

- It immobilizes the added water (ice) and binds it inside meat.
- It coats the particles of fat with a fine layer of protein so they don't clump together.

Proteins are also extracted from collagen rich tissues (skin, sinews, membranes) during the comminution process forming the protein solution. This solution can coat fat particles as well although it is less stable than the *myosin* solution. When heat is applied, collagen shrinks and forms a gelatin which results in some fat particles losing their protective coat. During heat processing the layer of protein solution that covers the fat particles coagulates and firmly entraps them into a newly created lattice. This prevents fat particles from unifying with each other. The ice which was added during cutting is absorbed by meat and the protein solution.

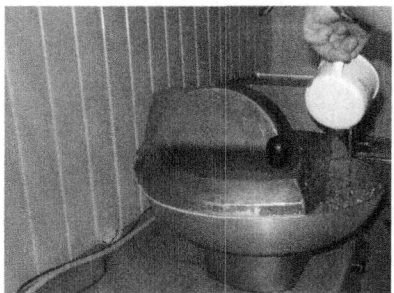

Photo 4.5 Rotating knives generate heat.

Photo 4.6 Flaked ice or cold water is added to control emulsion temperature.

Often more than one sausage type is produced at the same time, for example hot dog, frankfurter or bologna sausage. In this instance the emulsified mixture becomes a sausage mass *base* that may be used for different sausages. Of course besides salt and nitrite no other ingredients are added when making the base.

Lean meat can be cut manually into desired size pieces or ground through a coarse grinder plate. The fat can be diced into 1/8" or larger cubes. Those bigger parts will become the show meat in a finished sausage. Emulsified sausage base is mixed with other ingredients and stuffed into casings. Ingredients such as olives, pistachio nuts, and whole peppercorns may be added as well.

Mixing - for sausages processed with a grinder

Mix all ingredients with a cup of cold water and pour over minced meat. Start mixing, gradually adding flaked ice or cold water until a well mixed mass is obtained. We have been making wieners and frankfurters long before food processors came to be and there is no reason why we can't process them in the same way again.

Stuffing. Stuff hot dogs or frankfurters into sheep casings making 4-5 " (10-12 cm) links. Hang them for 1 hour at room temperature to dry out the casings and then place the sausages in a smokehouse. The smoking step is very important during commercial manufacturing as sausages such as hot dogs or frankfurters are skinless (no casings). They are stuffed into cellulose casings and then smoked. This creates a hardened surface which becomes a sort of artificial casing.

After smoking and cooking sausages go through the machine that cuts cellulose casings lengthwise and then the casing is peeled off. The hardened surface of the sausage is strong enough to hold a sausage mass in one piece. At home the sausages are stuffed into sheepskin casings which are tender and edible. and it is entirely up to you whether to remove the casings or not. If it comes off clean (no meat attached) and easy you may remove it. A skinless fresh sausage can be produced by stuffing meat into cellulose casings. The sausage is then frozen and the casing stripped off.

Smoking. Freshly stuffed sausages are left for 1-2 hours at room temperature or in a warm smokehouse at around 50° C (122° F) without smoke. The purpose of this step is to dry out the casings which should feel dry or tacky to the touch. We all know very well that we should not smoke wet meats or sausages. Sausages are smoked at 60-70° C (140-158° F) until a reddish-brown color is obtained.

Cooking. Cooking time depends directly on the temperature when the smoking has ended. At home conditions they will be submerged in hot water at 75° C (167° F). Frankfurters are thin sausages and 15 minutes cooking time is plenty. Keep in mind that they have been smoked at 60-70° C (140-158° F) for about 30 minutes and are already warm and partly pre-cooked. If a sausage diameter is larger, let's say 60 mm Mortadella, you may cook it at 75–78° C (167–172° F) for 90 minutes. A very large bologna sausage may be smoked for 3-5 hours and cooked for 5 hours more. A rule of thumb dictates 10 min for each 1 cm (3/8") of diameter of the sausage. There is no need for estimating time when a thermometer is used and cooking stops when the internal temperature of the sausage reaches 69-70° C (155-158° F). The majority of sausages are cooked at 80° C (176° F), using this temperature will shorten the cooking time.

Cooling (applies to all cooked sausages)

Immerse sausages in cool water. You may have to change the water once or twice depending on the size of the container and the size of production. If possible shower them or dip them very briefly with hot water to remove any grease on the surface. Hang sausages and wipe off any fat with a wet cloth. The reason for cooling is to bring the temperature down outside the Danger Zone (50-30° C, 122-86° F) where most bacteria find favorable conditions to grow. Although the cooking process kills 99% of bacteria, nevertheless new bacteria which are present all around will start multiplying again on the surface of the sausage. It is in our interest to bring the temperature below 30° C (86° F) as soon as possible. The sausages can be hung between 25-30° C (77-86° F) as at those temperatures moisture and heat evaporate from the surface rapidly. Then the sausages may be placed in a refrigerator.

Storing (applies to all cooked sausages)

Store in refrigerator or freeze for later.

Spices and additives. Aromatic seeds such as cloves, ginger, allspice, cinnamon, and nutmeg are commonly added to emulsified sausages. Other popular spices are white pepper, coriander and celery seed. The following additives can be used in emulsified products: non fat dry milk, starch, soy protein isolate or concentrate, egg whites, phosphates and ascorbates.

Liver Sausages

Liver sausages can be classified as:

- Regular liver sausages - coarsely comminuted through 5 mm grinder plate.
- Delicatessen type liver sausages - finely comminuted through 2 mm grinder plate and emulsified.
- Pâtés - liver sausages which are not stuffed, but placed in molds and baked or cooked in water. Molds are often lined with pastry and pâtés are covered with decorations and gelatin.

Liver is an organ that works hard by filtering blood and as an animal grows older, the liver becomes darker and might develop a slightly bitter taste. Think of it as if it were a filter that would become dirtier in time, the difference is that not the dust, but atoms of heavier materials like iron or copper will accumulate in time within its structure. Calf are slaughtered at the age of 4 months, a pig at 6 months, but a cow may live a few years. Because it is older the cow's liver and blood are darker and will induce a darker color to a finished sausage. All livers are suitable, however, their quality varies:

Liver source	Description
Veal	Excellent. Light color, great taste, more expensive.
Pork	Very good.
Lamb and goat	Good. Up to 50% can be mixed with pork liver.
Beef	Poor. Can be mixed with other livers but should not account for more than 25% of the total liver mass. Dark color.
Goose	Excellent.
turkey, duck	Good. Can be mixed with pork liver in any proportions.
Chicken	Poor, slightly bitter. Mix with pork liver.
Rabbit	Very good. Can be mixed with pork liver in any proportions.
Venison and wild game	Acceptable.

Liver must NOT be cooked. In many recipes liver is cooked briefly (blanched) in hot water for up to 5 min to remove any leftover blood but there is no real need for that. Blanching will cook some of the liver proteins and less of them would be available for emulsifying fat and water. Instead, liver can be rinsed and soaked in cold water for one hour to get rid of any traces of blood and remaining gall liquid. Soaking liver in milk is an old remedy for the removal of some of the liver's bitterness which can be noticeable in beef liver. Fresh liver tastes better than a frozen one.

Composition of a Liver Sausage

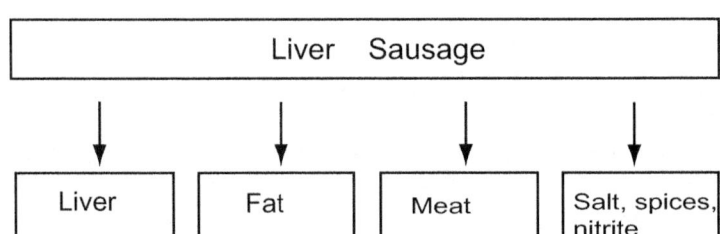

Fig. 4.1 Composition of a liver sausage.

Meat Selection

Meats used for commercially made liver sausages are first cured with sodium nitrite to obtain a pinkish color and the characteristic cured meat flavor. Sodium nitrite has some effect on extending the shelf life of the product and for that reason alone it is used by commercial processors. Liver sausages made at home in most cases employ meats that are not cured with sodium nitrite and the color of the sausage will be light yellow. That will largely depend on the type of liver and spices used.

It is advantageous, especially when making coarse type liver sausage, to use meats with a lot of connective tissues such as pork head meat, jowls (cheeks) or skin. Those parts contain a lot of collagen which will turn into gelatin during heat treatment. During subsequent cooling this gelatin will become a gel and that will make the sausage more spreadable with a richer mouthful texture. Meats commonly used in commercial production are pork head meat, jowls, meat trimmings and skin. Although pork head meat may not appeal to most people as a valuable meat, it is high in fat and connective tissues and contains more meat flavor than other cuts. For those reasons it is a perfect meat in liver or head cheese production.

If skinless pork jowls or skinless head meat is used about 5-10% of skins are added to the meat mass. Keep in mind that too many skins may make the texture of your sausage feel rubbery. Although tripe has practically no meat binding nor water holding properties, it is a nutritious material. About 10% cooked and finely ground beef tripe can be added to liver sausage. As the tripe is white, the sausage will develop a lighter color too. As long as the proper proportion of liver and fat are observed the remaining meats can be of any kind: pork, beef or veal.

Fat

Liver sausages contain a large percentage of fat (20-40%) which largely determines their texture and spreadability. If pork fat is used it makes no big difference whether a hard fat (back fat), soft fat (belly) or other fat trimmings are utilized. Vegetable oil may be mixed with liver and fat as well. Beef fat or pork flare fat (kidney) are not commonly used as they are hard and not easy to emulsify. To make fine spreadable liver sausage the fat should be dispersed in the liquid state at warm temperatures.

To achieve a final chopping temperature of around 95° F (35° C), fat or fat trimmings are usually poached at 176° F (80° C). Then when still warm they are ground and mixed without delay with liver, lean meat and spices together.

Salt, Spices and Other Ingredients

Liver sausages contain less salt than other sausages, the average being 12-18 g (1.2-1.8%) of salt per 1 kg of meat. Those sausages are of a much lighter color and for that reason white pepper is predominantly used. Most liver sausages are not smoked so there is no need to use nitrite. Occasionally after cooking liver sausages are cold smoked for a short time to add some smoky flavor. This short process has no effect on the preservation of the product which happens to be highly perishable.

Fresh onions are frequently used in home made liver sausages but are a poor choice in canned products and can create a sour taste. Onion's taste is greatly improved when the onion is fried in a little fat until glassy and golden. Milk or sweet cream is often added for a milder taste. Like in other sausages sugar may be added to offset the salty taste. Liver likes aromatic spices such as nutmeg, mace, allspice, marjoram, white pepper, sweet paprika and ginger. Vanilla is often added to create an aromatic sweet taste. Port or brandy are often added.

Home Production

Precooking meat. Meats (but no liver) are precooked in water and then ground/emulsified. Commercial plants cure meats with sodium nitrite regardless whether they will be smoked or not. Home made sausages are usually not treated with sodium nitrite. Pork skins are cooked at 85-90° C (185-194° F), when properly done they should hold their shape but you should be able to put your finger through them. If overcooked they will break into pieces. Fats and other meats are cooked at 85-90° C (185-194° F) until softer or meat reaches 70° C (158° F) internal temperature. *Don't discard leftover meat stock,* it can be added to the meat mass during emulsifying or grinding (about 0.1 liter - 0.2 liter, or 1/2 cup per 1 kg of meat).

Grinding. Warm pre-cooked meat should be minced with a small grinder plate 3-5 mm (1/8-3/16"). Liver is ground cold. As it contains a lot of water and blood, ground liver is easily emulsified.

Emulsifying. The sausage will have a more delicate texture when grinding is followed by emulsifying. If no food processor is available, grind meats and liver twice through the fine grinder plate. As raw liver is a natural emulsifier, this task is greatly simplified. During the comminution process the fat cells become ruptured and the free fat is released. Fat does not dissolve in water or mix with it well. *The purpose of emulsion is to bond free fat, meat and water together so they will not become separated.* Ground meats are emulsified in a kitchen food processor until a smooth paste is obtained. Liver is emulsified *separately* until air bubbles appear on the surface. Even if meat and fat are ground only, it is a good idea to at least emulsify the liver. If emulsification is not done right, the finished product might display pockets of fat. To prevent fat deposits experienced sausage makers gently massage warm sausages between their thumb and index fingers.

Mixing. Meat, fat and liver are mixed together with salt and spices, either manually or in a food processor. Between 10-20% meat stock may be added now. The resulting meat mass should be warm (35-40° C, 95-104° F) and not too dense.

Stuffing. The casings are filled rather loose and can be stuffed with a stuffer or a funnel. Beef middles or natural hog casings are often used, synthetic waterproof casings are fine but will not allow smoke to go through.

Photo 4.7 Stuffing liver sausages. Liver sausages are usually made into a ring.

Liver sausages are usually stuffed using a stuffer, however, when the sausage mass is thin they can be stuffed with a ladle and funnel.

Photo 4.8 Filling casings.

Times between grinding/emulsifying, mixing and stuffing should be kept to the minimum. The temperature of the sausage mass should stay at least at 35° C (95° F). Below this temperature fat particles will clump together. That prevents them from being properly coated by emulsified liver protein and increases the risk of fat separation during the cooking process.

Cooking. Liver sausages are poached at 176° F (80° C). When stuffed in natural casings, liver sausage release flavor and a little fat to cooking water. The resulting stock is usually saved for making soup.

Photo 4.10 Checking internal temperature.

Photo 4.9 Cooking sausages.

Cooling. Sausages are usually rinsed with tap water and then placed in cold water. Then they are spread on the table to cool.
Finely comminuted liver sausage may be gently massaged at this stage between the thumb and index finger. This will prevent the possibility of accumulating pockets of fat inside of the sausage. When the sausages are cool, they are placed in a refrigerator.

Photo 4.11 Cooling liver sausages.

Smoking. Once the sausages have cooled down to 30° C (86° F) they are sometimes submitted to a short (30-60 min) cold smoking process. The sausage acquires a golden color and smoky flavor. Additionally its shelf life will increase by a day or two.

Storing. Liver sausages must be refrigerated but can be frozen.

Kosher Liver Sausages. People who object to eating pork on religious reasons can still make liver sausages utilizing poultry and beef livers and replacing pork fat with oil. The rules of the game remain the same: to make a quality sausage you need liver, fat (oil), meat and spices. There is no need to worry about fat particles clumping together at below 35° C (95° F) as oil will remain in its liquid state.

Pâtés (French for "pie") is a type of a meatloaf whose composition resembles a liver sausage. Pâtè is baked in the oven or placed in molds which are inserted in a bigger dish filled with water and then baked. Some are placed in molds lined up with pastry.

Foie Gras (in French "fat liver") is a top quality pâté which is made with 80% of goose or duck liver with no other meats added.

Blood Sausages

Blood sausages have been made for thousands of years and every country has its own recipes. Blood sausage is without doubt the most under appreciated sausage of all. Unfortunately many of us display a preconceived opinion on some products. When they hear blood sausage they imagine that blood is bad and they will not even consider to try it. However, they go to a restaurant, order a medium rare steak and lick every drop of blood that remains on the plate.

Blood sausages were originally the first sausages that were made after pig slaughter. They were made from inexpensive raw materials such as pork head meat, jowls, tongues, groins, skins, pork or veal lungs, pork liver, beef and lamb liver, pork snouts, beef and liver lips, udders, beef and lamb tripe, veal casings, pork stomachs, pork heart, boiled bone meat and of course blood. All those cuts spoil easily, especially blood which in addition coagulates rapidly. This way every part of the animal was utilized and a highly nutritional product was made. In times of war and other hard times when meat was scarce, fillers were added to increase the volume of the sausage. Blood sausages can be divided into:

- Sliceable blood sausages - less than 10% blood, firm texture, often eaten cold, and of light color.
- Non-sliceable sausages - 30-60% blood, softer texture, eaten hot and darker.

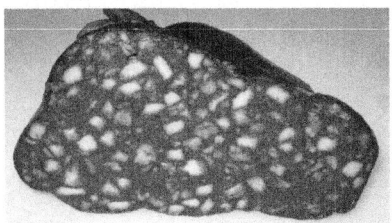

Photo 4.12 Sliceable blood sausages with diced fat.

Photo 4.13 Blood sausage with buckwheat grouts. Sliceable, but usually served hot.

Photo 4.14-left. Blood sausages with filler material can be sliced but are usually served hot.

Smoking blood sausages is not common. Blood sausages are often consumed cold but they taste better when fried or baked.

White Blood Sausage

A white blood sausage is made from pork *without* blood. It is just another version of a cooked sausage that in addition to meat, contains a large proportion of a filler material. The sausage is popular in countries such as England (White Pudding), France (Boudin Blanc), Poland (Biala Kaszanka), USA (Boudin Blanc, Cajun Style from Louisiana), Spain (Morcilla Blanca) or German (Weiss Blutwurst).

Photo 4.15 White blood sausage (no blood added) with rice.

Composition of Blood Sausage

Different cultures and/or regions have their own versions of blood sausage. These recipes are generally variable takes on a similar theme. The main ingredients are blood, fat, meat trimmings and usually a filler material. All of these are typically mixed together and stuffed into a casing. There are no rules for choosing the amount of blood or other materials. All combinations result in a good sausage.

Meat. In short a blood sausage is composed of pork or beef blood, pork fat and pork meat that often includes offal trimmings such as liver, snouts, hearts or skins. The whole is spiced and stuffed into a casing. When pork or lamb tongues are included, the product is known as tongue and blood sausage. In most cases a filler material will also be added.

Fat. Back fat is the best as it is hard and less likely to smear. Fat from pork butt and jowl fat are hard fats but belly fat (bacon) is soft. You can use any little fat pieces and fat trimmings. Sliceable blood sausage (without fillers) looks much nicer with visible pieces of white fat in it. To achieve this effect pork back fat should be cut into 4-5 mm (about 3/16") cubes which should be blanched briefly (5 min) in hot water (90-95° C, 194-203° F). This seals the surface of fat cubes and prevents blood from entering and discoloring it.

Skins. Skins are a very important ingredient as they contain a lot of collagen which will turn into gelatin during heat treatment. During subsequent cooling this gelatin becomes a gel that creates a better texture of the sausage. In sliceable blood sausages which are usually consumed cold this will positively contribute to the sliceability of the sausage. In non-sliceable sausages (with fillers and consumed hot) the gel will add firmness to the sausage.

Fillers. Many countries have their own traditionally used fillers that are combined with blood. The typical fillers are: buckwheat groats, barley, bread crumbs, rice, semolina flour, oats, potatoes, corn flour, onions, apples, raisins and more. Cream, milk and eggs are often added.

The addition of filler material makes a sausage very economical. Filler material such as rice, barley or buckwheat groats must be pre-cooked. Groats can be found in supermarkets but they have been factory processed and are ill suited for making blood sausages. The real natural groats can be ordered from online distributors such as the Sausage Maker or Bulk Foods. Many recipes call for oatmeal, but don't confuse this with instant oats which are served for breakfast. For sausages we use steel cut oats which are tough groats which must be soaked overnight. They can be pre-cooked as well but don't make them mushy. With such a variety of filler materials, meats and spices that can be chosen, it is hardly surprising to see the huge number of recipes floating around.

Blood. Blood from any animal including poultry can be used, although pig and cow bloods are most often used. Pork blood is a better choice as its color is lighter. The more blood, the darker the sausage. When blood is heated it becomes thicker and wonderfully binds other materials together. The amount of blood in a sausage can vary from 5%-60%, on average around 30%. Blood coagulates easily and is stirred frequently when collected during the slaughter. It must be used within 1-2 days and should be cold when mixed with other ingredients. Before use it must be stirred again and filtered through a cheese cloth, otherwise the sausage may contain solid lumps. Blood is a great food for bacteria and it should be cooled down quickly and placed in a refrigerator. It is advisable to process blood no later than on the second day. If the refrigerator is capable of maintaining temperatures of 1° C (33° F), the blood may be kept for 2-4 days. Adding salt or nitrite is not effective in extending blood's shelf life but blood can be frozen for later use. Commercial producers add anticoagulation chemicals (trisodium citrate) to prevent the coagulation of blood.

Photo 4.16 Morcilla Lustre.

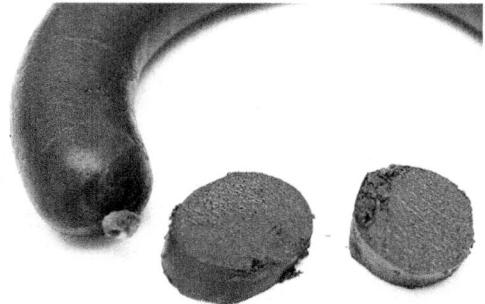

It may seem impossible, but Spanish "Morcilla Lustre" is made with 100% blood and ground spices. Being so thin the spiced blood is poured down the casing. After cooking in water the sausage becomes firm enough to be sliced and hold its shape.

It is not easy to obtain blood in a metropolitan area. Talk to the local butcher who may order frozen blood from meat purveyors. Blood can be purchased in Thailandese, Chinese, Japanese or Vietnamese stores. In European countries (not allowed in USA), dry blood powder is available for human consumption and is used for making blood sausages.

Salt, Spices and Other Ingredients. Blood sausages like highly aromatic spices such as: pepper, thyme, marjoram, caraway, pimento, cloves, nutmeg, allspice and coriander. Often apples, pine nuts, chestnuts, raisins and cream are added.

Onions. Raw onions when supplied in a larger amount can impart a sourly taste to the product. To eliminate this problem, in most cases onions are fried in oil first until they become transparent-glassy looking and acquire a golden color. In Spain it is a common practice to boil chopped onions before processing.

Photo 4.17 Buckwheat groats. Barley is also often used.

Photo 4.18 Buckwheat groats added to water.

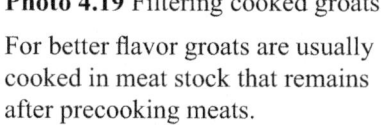

Photo 4.19 Filtering cooked groats.

For better flavor groats are usually cooked in meat stock that remains after precooking meats.

Manufacturing process

1. Cooking. Meat and filler material are pre-cooked before stuffing. The fat is not cooked but only scalded and diced into cubes. The blood is not pre-cooked.

2. Grinding. Except fat, all other pre-cooked meats are cooled, cut manually or ground through 1/8" (3 mm) plate and mixed together.

3. Mixing. Diced fat, blood, salt, and spices are added and everything is mixed together.

4. Stuffing. The blood sausage mass is much softer than the mixture for regular sausages. It can be stuffed with a stuffer or ladled into the casing through any suitable funnel. Traditionally blood sausages were stuffed into beef bungs or hog middles but any natural or synthetic casings will do. Prick any visible air pockets with a needle otherwise the sausages will swim up to the surface during cooking.

5. Cooking. The sausages are cooked in water at 80° C (176° F) for about 35-45 minutes, depending on the diameter. If they raise to the surface, remove air pockets with a needle.

6. Cooling. Chill in cold water, wipe off the moisture and store in a refrigerator.

Photo 4.20 Adding blood to groats.

Photo 4.21 Frozen blood.

Photo 4.22 Partially frozen blood is ground and mixed with spices.

Fig. 4.1 - right. Sausages with a large proportion of blood are easier to stuff using a ladle and funnel.

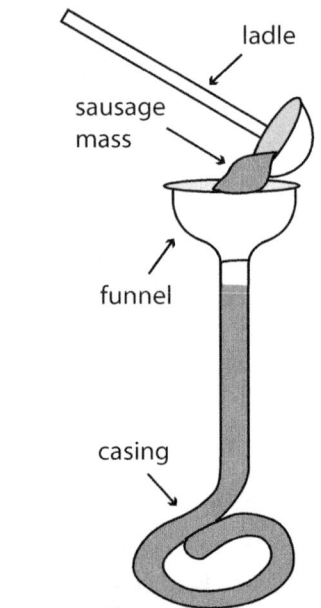

Photo 4.23 Stuffing blood sausages. If an excessive amount of blood is added to a sliceable sausage, solid chunks of meats will have a tendency to sink down and accumulate in one area. Sausages with filler material don't face this problem as the filler material acts like a sponge.

Photo 4.24 Cooked blood sausages.

Head Cheeses and Meat Jellies

In English, the name *head cheese* doesn't sound appealing which prevents many people from trying the product. In other languages it sounds much more appealing without the word *"head"* being part of the name. In German it is "sulz", in Polish "salceson." When vinegar is added, it is called "souse" and this already sounds much better. Head cheese, brawn, or souse are not cheeses, but rather jellied loaves or sausages that may or may not be stuffed into a large diameter casing. They can be easily found in places that cater to Central Europeans, Eastern Europeans and Italians.

Traditionally head cheese was made entirely from the meat of the head of a hog, cured and stuffed in large beef bungs or in pork stomachs. We may find this choice of meat today less appealing, forgetting at the same time the fact that pork head meat is highly nutritional and flavorsome.

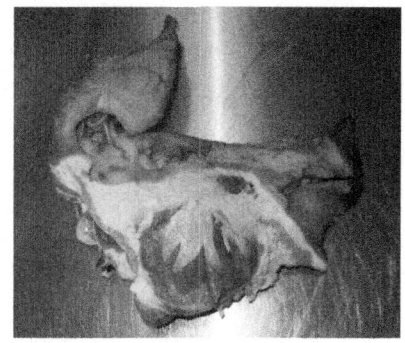

Photo 18.1 Pork head.

Persons living in metropolitan areas cannot buy pork head anyhow but still can make a great tasting product by using pork picnic and pigs feet. Nowadays head cheese can include edible parts of the feet, tongue, and heart. Many of us have made a head cheese before without even realizing it, although pork head meat was not a part of the recipe.

Every time we cook meat stock or chicken soup based on bones we are making a weak version of a head cheese. The reason the soup does not become a meat jelly is because there is too much water in it.

If this stock would simmer for a long time, enough water will be lost, and the resulting liquid when cooled will solidify and become a jelly. In the past after the first and second World War, or even in most countries today people had no opportunity to buy a commercially made gelatin. And this is why those unappealing cuts of meat like pork head, jowls, skins, hocks, legs and fatty picnic legs started to shine.

You cannot make real head cheese by using noble cuts like hams, tender loins or other tender lean meats. Those cuts do not contain enough connective tissues (collagen) in order to make natural gelatin. *You can use them, but a commercial grade gelatin must be added* and of course the taste and flavor of the finished product will be less satisfactory, although the resulting jelly will be very clear. Making head cheese is quite easy as the procedure does not involve the use of specialized equipment like a grinder or stuffer. Every kitchen contains all utensils that will be needed.

Types of Head Cheeses

- Regular head cheese - pork head meat, jowls, skins, snouts, pigs feet, gelatin.
- Tongue head cheese - in addition to the above mentioned meats the tongue is added. Cured with salt and nitrite in order to develop a pink color.
- Blood head cheese - head cheese made with blood. Such a head cheese is much darker in color.
- Souse - a head cheese to which vinegar has been added. Similar to sulz but not limited to pig's feet only. Most people eat head cheese with vinegar or lemon juice anyway, so it comes as no surprise that vinegar would be added to head cheese. It also increases the keeping qualities of the sausage as all foods containing vinegar last longer. Souse contains more jelly than a regular head cheese. In addition pimentos, green peppers or pickles are often added for decoration. Both sulz and souse contain about 75% of meat, 25% of jelly and around 3% of vinegar.
- Sulz - original head cheese made of pigs feet with the bone in. Later bones were removed to facilitate slicing. This name can be found in some older books. It was made with pig's feet only, but often snouts and pig skins were added as well. Meat jellies made from pig's feet are still popular in many European countries, in Poland they are known as pig's feet in aspic (*Nóżki w Galarecie*).
- Head cheese, souse and sulz are all very similar, the main difference is that souse and sulz contain vinegar and more gelatin. Commonly used spices are: pepper, nutmeg, mace, allspice, cloves, marjoram, cardamom, onions, garlic, caraway, thyme, ginger.

Photo 4.26 German head cheese.

Manufacturing Process

Meat selection. Traditionally made head cheese requires meats with a high collagen content to produce a natural gelatin. Meat cuts such as pork head, hocks and skins are capable of producing a lot of natural gelatin. In addition tongues, hearts, snouts and skins are also used as filler meats. Commercially made products don't depend on natural gelatin and use commercially produced gelatin powder instead which is made from skins and bones anyhow.

Meats that were traditionally used for head cheeses were:

Pork heads (cured or not), split in half - boiled in hot water at about 90° C (194° F) until meat was easily removed from bones by hand. The raw heads should be first soaked for 1-2 hours in cold water to remove any traces of coagulated blood.

Pork hocks (cured or not) - boiled at about 90° C (194° F) until meat is easily removed from bones by hand.

Skins. Pork skin should be clean without any remaining hair or excess fat. They are cooked at 85-90° C (185-194° F) until soft, requiring a longer cooking time. Pork shanks with meat (picnic), cured or not - boiled in hot water at about 90° C (194° F) until soft.

Lean pork trimmings (cured or not) - boiled in hot water at about 90° C (194° F) until soft.

Hearts (cured or not) - boiled in hot water at about 90° C (194° F) until soft. Hearts are first cut open and any remaining blood is rinsed away in cold water. The heart is a very hard working muscle and will be of a dark red color due to its high content of *myoglobin*. It should be diced into small diameter pieces (1/4", 5-6 mm) otherwise it will stand out.

Tongues (cured or not) - boiled in hot water at about 90° C (194° F) until soft. Pork or beef tongues are very often used but the outer skin on the tongues must be removed due to its bitter taste. It is easily accomplished once the tongues are submerged for a few minutes in hot water.

Curing meats. Traditionally made products may employ meat curing with nitrite or not. If meats are not cured with sodium nitrite the product will be of grey color, a matter that is of a little concern to a hobbyist. Head cheeses are not smoked so there is no need for sodium nitrite at least for safety reasons.

Cooking meats and making broth. This is basically one easy process but certain rules must be observed. Head cheese differs from other sausages in that meats are cooked before stuffing:

- All meats, skin included are cooked until soft.
- Meat is separated from bones.

Meats should be covered with 1-2 inches of water and simmered below the boiling point for 2-3 hours. The skins should be boiled separately until soft, but still in one piece. When still warm, cooked meats should be removed from bones and cooled down.

The skins are cut into strips. The resulting meat broth should be filtered. The better clarity obtained, the better looking cheese head will be produced. The resulting aspic is fat free and rich in protein product. When too much water is added it is possible to end up with a broth that will contain not enough gelatin to set. This may be corrected by additional boiling of the meat stock. As more water evaporates from the stock, the resulting meat broth gets concentrated and becomes a jelly. If this does not work you will have to re-heat the weak jelly, strain it and add a packet of a commercial gelatin. Then re-arrange meats on a plate and pour the hot gelatin over them. This will become a serious issue if the meat was already stuffed into the casing.

When in doubt it is safer to add powdered gelatin straight from the beginning than to create unnecessary extra work for yourself. As an extra precaution you may test your meat broth before it is added to the casing. Place a small amount in a refrigerator and see whether it solidifies within one hour. If not enough collagen is present, for example mainly lean meats were used, little gelatin will be produced and the resulting meat stock will not solidify. For best results mix powdered gelatin with the existing meat broth and not with water. Water will dilute the flavor of the broth.

Photo 4.27 Cooking head.

Photo 4.28 The meat is separated from bones.

Photo 4.29 Cooked meat trimmings.

Photo 4.30 Cooking head cheeses.

Cutting meats. The grinder is not employed as this will extract proteins and will break the fat's structure. *As a result a cloudy stock will be obtained.* Meats are much easier to cut into smaller pieces when chilled. After they are cut it is a good idea to rinse them briefly in hot water as *this will eliminate unnecessary grease that would normally cloud the jelly.* Until this point the process of making head cheese or meat jelly has been the same. What differentiates them is that head cheese is stuffed into a casing and meat jelly is not.

Mixing. Meats are mixed with all other ingredients. Although the recipe provides the amounts for all ingredients, it is recommended to taste the mixture and refine the recipe if needed.

Do not mix meat and broth together before stuffing. The hot jelly will draw some of the juices out of the meat and the jelly will become cloudy. A good idea is to scald meat with hot water to remove any grease that might cloud the gelatin.

Stuffing. Head cheese was traditionally stuffed into pig stomach. Pig stomach is a one unit chamber of uniform oval shape with two easy to sew openings. Stomachs of a cow or a sheep are basically three stomachs in one unit. The shape of those stomachs is irregular and not easy to fill. After filling the stomach's opening had to be sewn with butcher's twine.

Photo 4.31 Washing stomachs.

In most cases stomachs you buy will be pre-washed. All you will need is to reverse them, scrape off the fat and wash them.

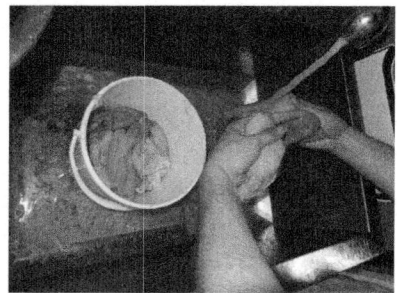

Photo 4.32 Turning stomachs inside out for cleaning.

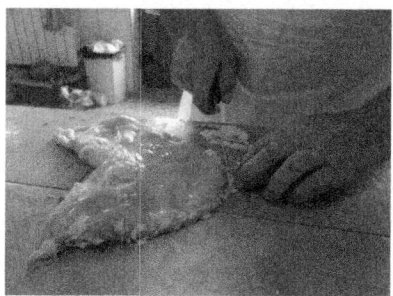

Photo 4.33 Scraping off fat.

Photo 4.34 Filling up the stomachs.

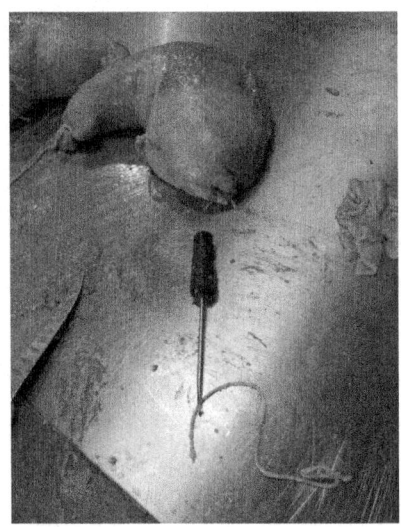

Photo 4.35 Basic tools are required.

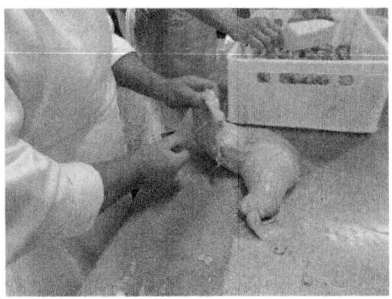

Photo 4.36 After filling the stomachs are stitched up and tied with twine.

Photo 4.37 Filled stomachs.

In the USA it will be hard for a hobbyist to find a pork stomach. The advice is to visit Asiatic meat markets. Nowadays, head cheese is stuffed into a large diameter synthetic casings, preferably a plastic one that will prevent loss of aspic during cooking. The tied or clipped at the bottom casing is held vertically and meat pieces are placed first. Then a gelatin from naturally produced meat broth or made from a commercial powder, is carefully poured down into the casing. This is normally done through a big funnel using a ladle. The casing is tied or clipped on the top and head cheese is ready for cooking.

Cooling. After cooking head cheese should be left at room temperature for a few hours. After that the head cheese is placed between two wooden boards. The top board is weighted and the sausage is stored overnight in a refrigerator. This permanently flattens the head cheese and produces the rectangular shape with rounded corners.

Photo 4.38 Cooked head cheeses cooling off.

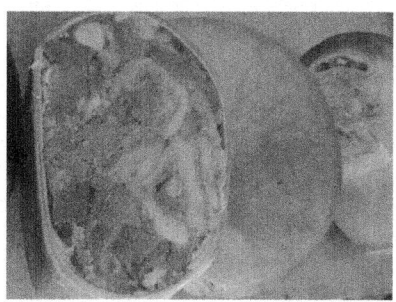

Photo 4.39 A head cheese is a big sausage.

Photo 4.40 Head cheeses cut into smaller portions.

Photo 4.41 Head cheese with a lot of aspic.

Photo 4.42 Head cheese with solid chunks of meat.

There are many variations of head cheeses. Some contain more jelly as more broth was added. Ingredients like red peppers, olives, garlic or vinegar may be added. They all share a common factor, they are delicious.

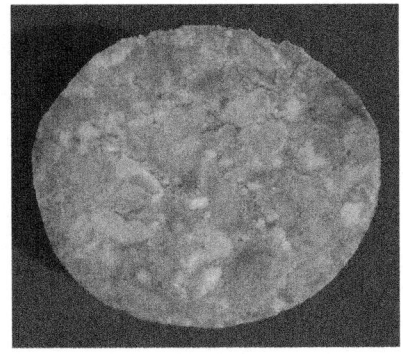

Photo 4.43 Head cheese with tongues.

Photo 4.44 Fine grind head cheese.

Meat jellies

Meat jellies are much easier to make than head cheeses as they don't have to be stuffed which greatly simplifies the procedure. In addition no secondary cooking is needed. Cooked meats are arranged on the bottom of the container, meat broth is carefully poured over it and left for cooling. It basically becomes a meat jelly.

Meat jelly although technically not a sausage, follows the same rules of production as a head cheese. They fit more into general cuisine and many fancy products can be created based on one's ingenuity and imagination. They are basically more refined products where the looks of the products play an important role. Because of that they contain solid chunks of lean "show meat" and are made with a commercial gelatin in order to obtain perfectly clear jelly. Different meats can be incorporated in meat jellies, for example fish fillets, skinless and boneless chicken breast, diced ham etc. As a rule meat jellies don't include low value meat products like skins, snouts, or hearts. Chicken breast or fish fillet will make a great show meat in any meat jelly.

Meat jellies are easily decorated:

- A thin layer of hot gelatin is placed in a form or deep plate and allowed to set in a cooler.
- Decorative items are placed on top of the set gelatin.
- A new layer of gelatin is poured on top and allowed to set in a cooler.
- Meat and the remaining gelatin are placed on top and allowed to set in a cooler.
- When ready for consumption the form is briefly placed in hot water which melts a thin layer of gelatin around it. Turning the form upside down will release the meat jelly with decorations being on top.

Decorative pieces such as slices of oranges, apples or hard boiled eggs are used. Herbs, cubed cheese, cracked pepper, slices of pickle, carrots, peas, corn, green scallions are often used in meat jellies.

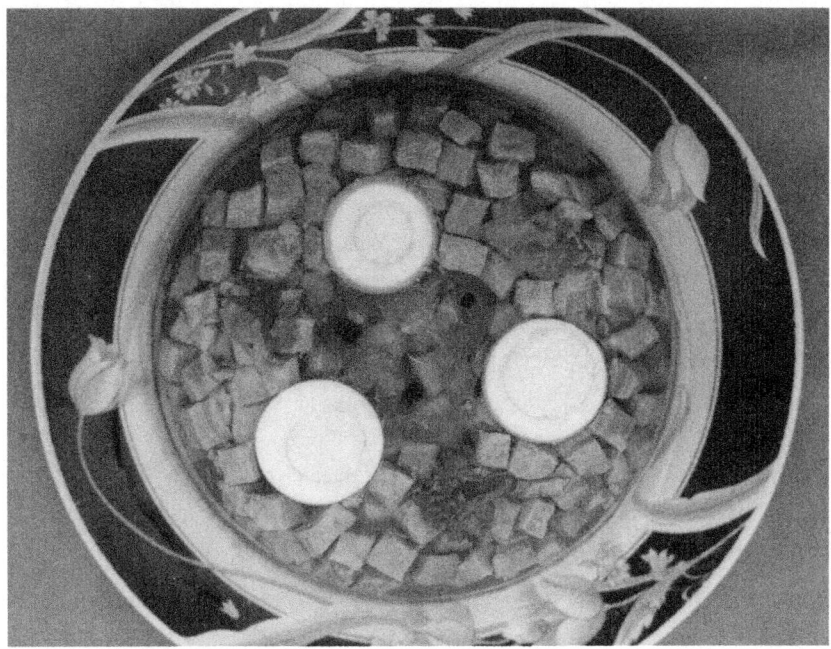

Photo 4.45 Diced ham jelly made with commercial gelatin. Sliced hard boiled eggs used for decoration.

Photo 4.46 Fish jelly made with commercial gelatin.

Gelatin

Natural gelatin is produced from meat stock such as the one used for head cheese manufacture. Natural stock will not be as clear as the one made by dissolving commercial gelatin powder with water. The main reason the natural stock is often cloudy is that it is boiled and not simmered. *Do not boil the stock, always simmer.* If you cook your stock gently, below the boiling point, the fat will not emulsify in water and the stock will remain clearer.

The natural gelatin that is obtained from boiled meats has a superior taste and flavor. The ingredients such as peppercorns, bay leaf, pimentos, and soup greens are often added to create a better flavor.

Clarifying stock. The natural stock can be filtered to obtain a clearer version.

1. Once when the stock cools down a little, the fat will accumulate on the surface and can be easily scooped up and discarded.

2. Then the liquid can be strained through a cheese cloth.

3. Refrigerate stock overnight. Skim any remaining fat off the top. Now you have crystal clear stock with great flavor.

Commercial gelatin is a powder that is obtained from skins, hooves, and other meat cuts that contain a lot of connective tissue. It has no flavor but is very clear and convenient to apply. A little salt and white vinegar should be added to give it some character. Packets of powdered gelatin are available in every supermarket and all that is required is to mix it with water. Gelatin use is not limited to meats and you can use it with fruits and juices as well. The size of the packet will dictate how much water is needed. Usually 1 part of gelatin to 6 parts water will produce a good jelly. If more powder is added the jelly will be much thicker.

To make a jelly:

1. Pour the gelatin into a container with cold water and let it stand until the gelatin absorbs the water. Do not stir.

2. Place this container inside another vessel filled with hot water.

3. Heat the water until the gelatin solution reaches 160° F (72° C).

Note: if gelatin solution is heated above 160° F, it will lose its binding power.

Useful Information

Head cheeses, liver sausages and blood sausages belong to a special group of products that incorporate less noble cuts of meat that will be much harder to sell to the public at least in their original form. What separates those products from other common sausages is the fact that meats are precooked before being stuffed into casings and then they are submitted to a hot water cooking process. Another peculiarity is that all those products are often made *without being stuffed into casings.*

- Head cheeses when placed in forms and boiled in water become meat jellies.
- Head cheese is usually eaten cold or at room temperature as a luncheon meat.
- Head cheese freezes very well.
- Diced meats must be washed with hot water to remove any fat particles from the surface and then drained. This will make them look sharp in jelly.
- Gelatin should be soaked in cold (room temperature) water for about 15 min to swell and then mixed with hot water.
- Commercial gelatin produces a very clean, transparent jelly. Traditionally made meat jelly may use natural gelatin (broth) as the looks of the product are less important. Lean cuts of meat such as hams, pork loins, chicken breast or fish fillet will look much better in a clean, commercially made gelatin. On the other hand the natural meat broth may be sometimes cloudy but has superior taste.
- Commercial gelatin packets come with instructions and are available in every supermarket, for example Knox® brand. If jelly does not want to set in because gelatin was made too thin, reheat your weak jelly, strain it and reinforce it with an extra packet of gelatin. Then pour your stronger and warmer gelatin over the meat.
- Meat jellies can be made of lean meats and will taste good even if little salt is added (1.0 %)
- The gelatin is often made with wine, brandy and other spirits to create a high quality product.
- Show meat, for example tongues, may be cured in order to develop a pink color.

Traditionally made head cheese or meat jelly may look less pretty but will be a product of much higher quality due to the following reasons:

- No chemicals are added.
- No water is pumped into meat which results in a stronger meatier flavor.
- It contains the natural broth. Commercially prepared gelatin is a combination of neutrally flavored powder (natural glue) and water and natural broth is a combination of natural glue plus highly flavored meat stock that remains after cooking bones. Upon cooling this gelatin becomes a jelly and accounts for about 30% of the total weight of the product. And 30% of meat broth tastes much better than 30% of water.

Fermented Sausages

Although the processing steps for making fermented sausages may look faniliar, however, under closer examination it becomes clear that they have to be finely tuned to new safety requirements. In many cases fermented sausages are not submitted to heat treatment at all and *that separates them from other sausage types.* Clearly to make raw meat safe to consume requires different measures and to understand the subject better it is necessary to become familiar with two new concepts of vital importance: Aw - water activity and pH - acidity.

pH -The Measure of Food Acidity

The term "pH" is a measure of acidity; the lower its value the more acidic the food. *Bacteria hate acidity and this fact plays an important role in the production and stabilization of fermented sausages.* Acidity may be natural as in most fruits for example lemon, or added as in pickled food. The acidity level in foods can be increased (lowering pH) by adding lemon juice, citric acid, or vinegar, or lowered (increasing pH) by adding baking soda, milk or water.

All bacteria have their own preferred acidity level for growth, generally around neutral pH 7.0 which is pure water. Solutions with a pH less than 7 are said to be *acidic* and solutions with a pH greater than 7 are basic or *alkaline.*

    The pH value of 4.6 is the division between high acid foods and low acid foods. Low acid foods have pH values higher than 4.6. They include red meats, seafood, poultry, milk, and all fresh vegetables except for most tomatoes. Acidity in meats varies between pH5.1 and pH6.8. The thermal resistance of microorganisms decreases as the pH of their medium is lowered. As the pH of foods can be adjusted this procedure becomes a potent weapon for the control of bacteria. Bacteria will not grow when the pH is below the minimum or above the maximum limit for a particular bacteria strain. Most bacteria, particularly *Clostridium botulinum*, will not grow below pH 4.6.

Water Activity (Aw)

All microorganisms need water and the amount of water available to them is defined as water activity. Water activity (Aw) is an indication of how tightly water is "bound" inside of a product. It does not say how much water there is, but how much water is *available* to support the growth of bacteria, yeasts or molds.

    A simple scale is used to classify foods by their water activity and it starts at 0 (bone dry) and ends on 1 (pure water).

    Freshly minced meat possesses a very high water activity level around 0.99, which is a breeding ground for bacteria. Adding salt to meat drops this value immediately to 0.96-0.98 (depending on the amount of salt), and this already creates a hurdle against the growth of bacteria. Although the addition of salt to meat does not force water to evaporate, it does something similar: it immobilizes free water and prevents it from reacting with anything else, including bacteria. It is like stealing food from bacteria, the salt locks up the water creating less favorable conditions for bacteria to grow and prosper.

As we add more salt more free water is immobilized, but a compromise must be reached as adding too much salt will make the product unpalatable. It may also impede the growth of friendly bacteria, the ones which work with us to ferment the sausage.

Below certain Aw levels microbes cannot grow. United Stated Department of Agriculture guidelines state that:

"A potentially hazardous food does not include . . . a food with a water activity value of 0.85 or less."

A meat inspector can check any food with portable Aw tester and if the reading is below 0.85 the food, for example beef jerky, is safe.

Water activity of some foods	
Pure water	1.00
Fresh meat & fish	0.99
Bread	0.99
Salami	0.87
Aged cheese	0.85
Jams & jellies	0.80
Plum pudding	0.80
Dried fruits	0.60
Biscuits	0.30
Milk powder	0.20
Instant coffee	0.20
Bone dry	0.00

Effects of temperature, acidity (pH) and moisture (Aw) on bacteria behavior:

Name	Temperature in ° C			Min pH	Min Aw
	Min	Optimum	Max		
Salmonella	7	35 - 37	45	3.8	0.94
Cl.botulinum	3	18 - 25	45	5.0	0.97
Cl.perfringens	12	43 - 47	50	5.5	0.93
Staph.aureus	6	37	48	4.2	**0.85**
Campylobacter	30	42	45	4.9	0.98
Listeria	-1.5	37	45	4.4	0.92
E.coli	7	37	46	4.4	0.95
Shigella	7	35-37	47	4.0	0.91
Bacillus	4	30 - 37	55	4.3	0.91
Below min pH and min Aw bacteria will not grow.					

Controlling pH and Aw is crucial when making fermented products, for the purpose of this book it is enough to know that bacteria hate high acidity (low pH) and low water levels (Aw). The whole science of food drying is based in the principle of Aw water activity. From the above table it can be seen that except *Staphylococcus aureus*, all other bacteria (spoilage and pathogenic) will not grow below Aw 0.91.

Types of Fermented Sausages

- Fermented Dry Sausages
- Fermented Semi-Dry Sausages
- Chemically Acidified Fermented Sausages
- Non-Acidified Fermented Sausages

Fermented Dry Sausages

These are classical dry sausages which we associated with Italian salami. The technology of making dry sausages relies on *drying*. They are done after losing about 35% of moisture. When stored at 15° C, (60° F) 70-75% humidity, such a sausage will last for at least one year. Italian salami, Spanish salchichón or French Saucisson sec are typical examples. In other countries they are simply called salami, for exammple Hungarian or Polish salami. They are made with a very small amount of sugar to jump start fermentation or none at all. This why have such a superior flavor that depends mainly on the breakdown of sugars, fats and proteins during the fermentation and drying processes.

Traditionally produced fermented dry sausages do not develop a sourly taste and their flavor is mild and cheesy.

Fermented Semi-Dry Sausages

These are fast-fermented sausages that are made safe by acidification to pH 5.3 or less. In addition they must lose about 15% of moisture. The drying occurs during fermenting and cooking, so a dedicated dry room is not needed. Summer sausage, Lebanon bologna and Thuringer are examples of fermented semi-dry sausages. Most semi-dry types are cooked following fermentation and exhibit finer grind and lower pH (<4.8). A typical summer sausage process would include a fermentation period of 12-16 hours at 37.8° C (100° F), 98% humidity to a pH < 5.0, followed by a smoking/cooking cycle to a minimum of 60° C (140° F) internal temperature. Many products are shelf-stable, with limiting amounts of added sugars (to prevent secondary fermentation in the vacuum package) and fully cooked to 71-74° C (160-165° F) internal temperature.

Fermented semi-dry sausages exhibit a somewhat acidic sourly taste which is accepted in the USA, but is not popular in European countries.

Chemically Acidified Sausages

Commercial producers add chemicals such as Gdl (glucono-delta-lactone) or citric acid into a sausage mass to rapidly increase the acidity of the meat and to create an extra margin of safety. Unfortunately this introduces a sourly flavor. The entire process takes 6-7 hours versus 12-18 hours for fast-fermented semi-dry process or at least 1 month for traditionally produced salami.

Non-Fermented Dried Sausages

Some sausages are not fermented or acidified, yet shelf stable. They are made without cultures or acidulants (Gdl, citric acid) and no fermentation takes place. Generally after stuffing these sausages are partially cooked to 63° C (146° F) and then dried to a water activity of < 0.85 (Aw growth limit for *Staph. aureus*). Due to the higher pH these products must be dried to a lower water activity than fermented products to achieve shelf stability. Non-fermented dried sausages are also known as non-fermented salamis.

Sausage Flavor

Dry sausages made with salt and *pepper only* will have a wonderful mellow cheesy flavor *which is created in time by the reaction of bacteria with meat.* The true salami flavor of a slow-fermented sausage is created by the breakdown of sugars, fats and proteins through the fermentation and drying process. These reactions are products of microbiological action of color and flavor forming bacteria, which need *sufficient time* to develop a true salami flavor.

The metabolism of sugar by bacteria and resulting lactic acid production is directly responsible for the tangy and sour taste in fast-fermented sausages.

Fast-fermented sausages will always exhibit this tangy and sourly flavor as bacteria don't receive sufficient time to work with meat. Additionaly the rapidly raising acidity inhibits their growth. To make up for the sourly flavor a a variety of spices, sugars, extracts and syrups can somewhat off set the acidity of the meat.

The tangy and sourly flavor is the result of fermentation. Food can only be fermented if it contains sugar, for example cabbage which contains about 3% sugar after fermenting becomes sauerkraut with a sourly flavor. Meat contains less than 1% sugar (glycogen) which is too little for any meaningful fermentation. If no additional sugar is added, such a sausage can stll be made safe by drying only and it will become a top quality salami. This, however, becomes a time consuming process that requires more knowledge and experience.

A question that may arise is, "why add sugar if it has a negative effect on sausage flavor?" The answer is that it prevents meat from spoiling, especially in initial hours of production of fast produced sausages. A fast-fermented sausage can be produced in 12 hours, but it may take 1-3 months to produce a dry sausage.

Photo 4.47 Spanish Salchichón - fermented dry sausage.

General Guidelines for Making Fermented Sausages

All tasks involved in the manufacture of fermented sausages must always be performed in such a way that meat safety is *never compromised.* A mistake in any of the processing steps can later spoil the sausage or bring harm to the consumer.

It is not possible to cover production of fermented sausages in one chapter, however, more information is available in "The Art of Making Fermented Sausages" by Stanley and Adam Marianski, the 270 page book which covers the subject in detail.

Meat selection. Only the best raw materials are chosen for making dry or semi-dry sausages. Any blood clots and glands must be removed as these may accumulate undesired bacteria. Those bacteria will then multiply during the curing or fermentation step and will affect the quality of the product. Meats must be well trimmed of gristle and sinews. Such defects are not apparent in emulsified sausages but will strike out in coarsely ground fermented sausages. Buying ground meat is not a good solution as it has the shortest life due to its large surface area and it has a large bacteria count. Different meats can be used to make fermented sausages: pork, beef, lamb, goat, venison, poultry or a combination thereof. In Germany fermented sausages are often made from equal amounts of pork and beef, in Poland pork is more popular. Hungarian, Italian, Spanish and French sausages contain mostly pork.

Fat. When making fermented sausages use pork back fat. It is hard, it has a higher melting point, and it tastes best. Soft fat (belly) smears easily and may adhere to the inner casing surface, clogging up the pores and affecting drying. It may also coat meat particles which will inhibit the drying process. Although soft fat is a poor choice for making sliceable sausages, it can be successfully used for making fermented spreadable sausages (Mettwurst, Teewurst), especially the ones with a fine grind. Make sure the fat is partially frozen before it is ground or cut. Fat contains little water (10-15%), so the sausage with a large proportion of fat will dry faster.

Salt

When making fermented sausages use between 2.5-3.5 % salt as this combined with nitrite is your first line of defense against undesirable bacteria. Almost all *regular* sausage recipes (fresh, smoked, cooked etc) contain 1.5-2% of salt which is added to obtain a good flavor. These amounts are *not high enough* to provide safety against bacteria and *there is no room for compromise.* Use 3.0-3.5% salt when making traditionally fermented dry sausages without starter cultures. For all other types use 2.5% common non-iodized salt.

Nitrates

You must not make fermented sausages without nitrite/nitrate as they provide protection against pathogenic bacteria.

Cure #1 (sodium nitrite) - use for fast-fermented sausages

Cure #2 (sodium nitrite and sodium nitrate) - use for slow-fermented products, as nitrite starts reacting with meat at low temperatures and nitrate guarantees a stable color during long term drying.

Sugar

Fresh meat contains very little glucose (0.08-0.1%), which is not enough for lactic acid bacteria to produce any significant amount of lactic acid. Adding sufficient amounts of sugar is of great importance for fast-fermented sausages which rely on acidity as a main safety hurdle. About 0.3-1% dextrose (glucose) must be introduced into meat when making a fast fermented product.

For slow-fermented sausages the amount of added sugar is much smaller (0.1 - 0.3%), as the microbiological safety is achieved by drying products and not by increasing acidity. Many traditional long dried sausages do not employ any sugars at all. In general, increasing sugar levels up to 1% decreases pH proportionally. In specific products (e.g. American pepperoni), limiting sugar to 0.5-0.75% creates adequate fermentation with no residual carbohydrate present after fermentation. *A lower pH is obtained with increasing temperature at the same sugar level.*

Amount of sugar in %	final pH
0.3	more than 5.0
0.5 - 0.7	less than 5.0
1.0	4.5

Glucose - also known as *dextrose,* is approximately 70% as sweet as sucrose. It is the simplest form of sugar and because of its simplicity it can be directly fermented into lactic acid by all lactic bacteria. It is the fastest acting sugar for lowering pH. As lowering pH is the main hurdle against bacteria growth *in fast-fermented sausages, dextrose is the sugar of choice.*

Sucrose - common sugar (also called saccharose) is composed of 50% glucose and 50% fructose and is the second fastest acting sugar. It can be used with Gdl in medium-fermented sausages. In slow-fermented sausages common sugar can be used as it has been used for hundreds of years. Usually a combination of dextrose and sugar is used as bacteria are able to immediately metabolise dextrose and produce lactic acid (acidity) to contribute to meat safety. After a short delay the bacteria consumes sugar which is needed to break down to glucose (dextrose), delaying the production of lactic acid.

Spices. Without a doubt *black pepper is the most popular spice* added to fermented sausages (0.2-0.3%, 2-3 g/kg). The most popular spices in the manufacture of fermented sausages are *pepper and garlic.* Spices added to the sausage also contribute to the flavor, more so in the case of fast-fermented products. Spices lose their aroma rapidly and their contribution to flavor in slow-fermented sausages is weaker.

Smoking

Smoking may or may not be utilized in the production of fermented sausages. Smoking imparts a different flavor, fights bacteria, (especially on the surface of the product) and thus prevents the growth of molds on fermented sausages. Mold is desired on some traditionally made Italian salamis and obviously smoking is not deployed.

It should be noted that *when making slow-fermented sausages only cold smoke should be applied* and its temperature should correspond to the fermentation or drying temperature present at a particular time. Semi-dry sausages which are of fast-fermented type, are fermented at higher temperatures. These sausages can be smoked with warmer smoke as they are subsequently cooked.

Starter Cultures

Although lactic acid bacteria are naturally present in meat, their quantity and qualities are hard to predict. In most cases they are of a hetero-fermentative type and that means that they not only produce lactic acid by metabolizing carbohydrates, but also create many different reactions which can produce unpleasant odors and affect the entire process. *Starter cultures are of a homo-fermentative type and will produce lactic acid only.*

The advantages of starter cultures are numerous:

- They are of known number and quality. This eliminates a lot of guessing as to whether there is enough bacteria inside the meat to start fermentation, or whether a strong curing color will be obtained.
- Cultures are optimized for different temperature ranges that allow production of slow, medium or fast-fermented products. Traditionally produced sausages needed three (or more) months to make, starter cultures make this possible within weeks.
- Production of fermented sausages does not depend on "secrets" and a product of constant quality can be produced year round in any climatic zone, as long as proper natural conditions or fermenting/drying chambers are available.
- They provide safety by competing for food with undesirable bacteria thus inhibiting their growth.

There are many manufacturers of starter cultures that are used in Europe and in the USA, for example cultures made by the Danish manufacturer "Chr. Hansen". Their products demonstrate superior quality and are easily obtained online. Some of the popular cultures are listed below:

Bactoferm™ T-SPX - slow-fermented culture for traditional fermentation profiles applying fermentation temperatures not higher than 24° C (75° F).

Bactoferm™ F-LC - bio-protective culture capable of acidification as well as preventing growth of pathogenic *Listeria monocytogenes*. Controlling *Listeria monocytogenes* is not easy as it is so widespread. The culture works in a wide temperature range. Low fermentation temperature <25° C (<77° F) results in a traditional acidification profile whereas high fermentation temperature 35-45° C (95-115° F) gives a US style product. *Use dextrose as this culture ferments sugar slowly.*

F-RM-52 - Fast culture targeted for fermentation temperatures 22-32° C (70-90° F).

LHP-Extra fast cultures for fermentation temperatures 26-38° C (80-100° F).

Mold-600 Bactoferm™ (formely **M-EK-4)** - White mold cultures for surface treatment.

When starter cultures are used, the fermentation temperature can vary from the minimum to the maximum setting recommended by the manufacturer and as long as we follow this advice the sausage will turn out fine. Technical information sheets provide the recommended temperatures for fermentation, however, *bacteria will also ferment at lower temperatures, just more slowly.* For example, the technical information sheet for T-SPX lists temperatures as 26-38° C (78-100° F), optimum being 32° C (89° F). T-SPX will ferment as well at 20-24° C (68-75° F) which is not uncommon for "European" style sausages and 48 hours or more is not atypical.

Fermentation

In simple terms *meat fermentation is spoilage of meat by bacteria.* If this process is left to itself, the meat will spoil. But if it is properly controlled the result is a fermented product. Meat fermentation is accomplished by lactic bacteria, either naturally present in meat or added as starter cultures. These bacteria feed on carbohydrates (sugars) and produce lactic acid and small amounts of other components.

The start of fermentation is nothing else but a war declaration by bacteria residing inside the meat and the stuffed sausage becomes the battlefront.

When a sausage is introduced into a fermentation chamber, the bacteria hold all cards in their favor:

- Warm temperature - inside of the "danger zone."
- Moisture - meat contains 75% water.
- Sugar (food) - little sugar is present in the meat itself (glycogen) but extra amounts are usually added.
- Oxygen, present in air. Food spoilage bacteria require oxygen to grow, but there are bacteria that thrive without oxygen.

When a sausage is stuffed *the only barrier that protects the meat from spoiling is salt and nitrite which were introduced during curing or mixing.* The selected meat always contains some bacteria and they will grow in time. There is a fierce competition among different groups of bacteria for food. Bacteria that are beneficial to us slowly but steadily gain the upper hand in this fight by eliminating the food spoilage and pathogenic types. "Survival of the fittest" at its best. The reason that beneficial bacteria get the upper hand in this war is that they are stronger competitors and they better tolerate exposure to salt, nitrite and decreased water levels.

The main product of fermentation is lactic acid and the main cause is an increased acidity of meat (lower pH). The more sugar that is metabolized by the lactic acid bacteria, the more lactic acid is produced and the higher acidity of meat is obtained. This increased acidity of meat known as pH drop, erects the barrier against the growth of spoilage and dangerous bacteria.

The speed of fermentation is due to temperature and higher temperatures produce faster fermentation. *How acidic the sausage becomes depends on the amount and type of sugar introduced.* If more sugar is added, a higher acidity (lower pH) is obtained and the sausage gains a more sourly flavor.

Fermentation stops when no more lactic acid is produced by bacteria. This happens when:

- No more sugar is available to lactic acid bacteria.
- There is not enough free water (Aw < 0.95) available to lactic acid bacteria. This can happen when a sausage dries too fast during fermentation due to low humidity and fast air speed.
- Temperature is lowered < 12° C (53° F), or the product is heated to more than 50° C (120° F).

As to when fermentation stops and drying begins, there is no easy answer especially in the case of slow-fermented products that are made with little sugar, which leads to a slow and small pH drop. pH will have to be periodically monitored and once it is at its lowest, it means that there is no more lactic acid production and no more fermentation. *The sausage pH, not the time, is the factor that determines when the fermentation is completed.* It should be noted that when yeasts and molds appear on the sausage during the drying process, "reversed" fermentation will take place as these microorganisms consume some of the lactic acid that was produced during fermentation. This will lower acidity (increase pH) further contributing to a milder flavor in the slow drying sausages. There are processors of dry products that limit the entire process to one long drying step.

Drying

Drying is normally performed at, 18 → 12° C (66 → 54° F) with decreasing humidity, from about 85% to 65-70%. Higher temperatures and humidity over 75% will promote the development of mold on the surface of the sausage. *Sausages dry from inside out* and to have a correct drying process there must be a balance between moisture diffusion towards the surface and moisture evaporation from the surface. If diffusion is faster than evaporation, moisture will accumulate on the surface of the sausage causing it to be slimy and yeasts and molds will follow. If evaporation is faster than diffusion, the outside surface area of the sausage will dry out and harden creating a barrier to subsequent moisture removal. As a result moisture will be trapped inside of the sausage creating favorable conditions for the growth of spoilage and pathogenic bacteria. Water activity can be lowered faster in a sausage which contains more fat than a leaner sausage. Meat contains about 75% of water but the water content of fat is only about 10-15%. A fatter sausage containing less meat also contains less water and will dry out faster.

Drying basically starts in the fermentation stage and is affected by the following factors:

- Humidity - higher humidity, slower drying.
- Temperature - higher temperature, faster drying.

Drying continues after the fermentation stage and more moisture is removed from the sausage. And the process continues until the desired amount of dryness is obtained.

The factors affecting drying:

- The length of the sausage has no influence on drying time.
- Sausages should be dried at a rate not higher than the moisture losing ability of the sausage.
- Traditionally made sausages have pH of about 5.3 and Aw about 0.88 at the end of the drying process.
- The drying chamber should not be overloaded as a uniform air draft is needed for proper drying and mold prevention.
- Air speed - higher air speed, faster drying.
- Casing type (pore size) - bigger pores, faster drying.
- Amount of fat - more fat in sausage, faster drying.
- Meat particle size - bigger size, faster drying.
- Sausage diameter - bigger diameter, slower drying.
- Sausage length does not affect drying.
- A medium diameter sausage should lose about *0.5-0.7% of its weight per day* when in a drying chamber.
- Load capacity of the drying room-fully loaded chamber will dry slower as air movement is restricted.
- Molds will develop more quickly if there is no air draft at all. Excessive drying hardens the surface and closes the casing pores.
- If the outside of the sausage becomes greasy, it should be wiped off with a warm cloth otherwise it may inhibit drying.

Storing

Fermented sausages (except spreadable sausages) can be stored at 10-15° C (50-59° F), <75% humidity. Spreadable sausages which are neither dried nor cooked, must be refrigerated.

Safety Hurdles

To protect fermented sausage from spoiling a combination of safety measures known as hurdles is implemented. For example the first hurdle is an application of salt and sodium nitrite which slows down spoilage and keeps pathogenic bacteria at bay. This first hurdle is a temporary one, and if we need to follow up with additional ones.

- Processing meats with a low bacteria count at low temperatures
- Curing with salt and nitrite/nitrate
- Lowering pH of the meat to < 5.3
- Lowering Aw (water activity) by drying to Aw< 0.91
- Using bio-protective cultures
- Smoking
- Cooking
- Spices
- Cleanliness and common sense

Air Dried Sausages

Air dried sausages such as Spanish chorizo or cold smoked and then air dried sausages conform to the same safety rules as fermented sausages. In many cases they are made without starter cultures and all safety hurdles as explained in this chapter must be obeyed. Fresh meat, processing at low temperatures and a high percentage of salt and sodium nitrite will offer protection in the initial stages of production. Then as the sausage keeps on drying it loses more moisture and becomes more stable in time. Needless to say the production of fermented and air dried sausages require more skill and knowledge on the part of a sausage maker.

Poultry Sausages

The most popular meats on the market are: chicken, turkey, duck and goose. This does not necessarily mean that chicken meat is superior to goose. Chicken occupies the # 1 spot as it is the most *profitable* poultry to raise. It needs less feed than other poultry types, its meat contains little fat and the bird is popular due to its egg producing capabilities. Poultry meat is fine for making emulsified sausages that would be cooked in water. The best example is a variety of poultry hotdogs and frankfurters that are carried in our supermarkets.

Chicken fat contains more water and less collagen structure than other fats which makes it soft and semi-liquid at room temperature due to its low melting point. When submitted to heat treatment, chicken fat will melt inside the sausage creating oily pockets and make the sausage seem like a fat product. For those reasons pork fat should be added to a sausage, but it cannot be classified as an all chicken sausage anymore.

Turkey is inexpensive and it has the biggest breast of all poultry. Turkey breast is a great cut for smoking. All parts of turkey can be used for sausages.

Goose and Duck. These birds are much fatter, especially the skin which contains a lot of attached fat. As skin contains a lot of collagen it can bind water and emulsify fats very well. Meats from those birds will make good sausages, in addition goose and duck livers are superior material for making liver sausages.

A basic formula: 45% poultry meat, 25% poultry skins, 10% poultry fat, 10% water, non-fat dry milk, starch, salt, spices.

Follow processing steps for emulsified sausage.

Fish Sausages

Fish is a cheap raw material which is easy to process. Fish products and sausages are popular in countries such as the Philippines, Thailand, Malaysia, Japan, and China. The products are often made into fermented fish paste and fish sauce which are used for general cooking. Rice is used as a filler and the source of carbohydrates for fermentation.

The benefits of making sausages from fish:

- Cheap raw material
- Easy to process
- All varieties can be used, including de-boned meat
- Healthy product

The disadvantages of making sausages from fish:

- Soft texture, fish need to be combined with pork fat, vegetable oil, other meats and fillers like starch, soy protein concentrate or carrageenan.
- Fish contain little myoglobin so treating white fish with sodium nitrite will not produce a pink color so typical in regular sausages.
- The final flavor tends to remain fishy even when other meats are added.

There was research done on making fermented fish sausages and the customer acceptance in order of preference follows below:

- Fish-pork, the highest score
- Fish-beef
- Fish-chicken

There are three types of products made from fish:

- Finely comminuted sausages in small diameter casings
- Fish hams made in casings of large diameter
- Fish jellies

Fish sausage manufacturing follows the general steps which are employed in making emulsified cooked sausages. In Europe, other countries, for example Poland, have also showed interest in utilizing less popular fish species for manufacture of fish sausages. It was discovered that a sausage of good quality was made when in addition to fish, pork, beef, eggs and starch were included in a recipe.

A hobbyist will process a few fish at the time and fillets and fish trimmings will be relatively clean. Processes like soaking and pressing or draining may be avoided altogether. A typical composition of a fish sausage is as follows: 67-68% water, 14-15% protein, 5-6% fat and 8-9% starch.

Wild Game

The definition of wild game covers large animals such as dear, elk, moose, bear, mountain goat, and smaller animals such as squirrel, rabbit, opossum, and wild birds. Meat from wild animals is very lean, dark in color, and often has a gamey flavor which some people find objectionable. Fat is known to carry a lot of this flavor and *as much of the fat as possible should be cut away.* As game meat contains very little fat to begin with, it is understood that smoking and cooking will produce a very dry product. The solution is to pork back fat or fat trimmings.

Any wild animal that eats meat is at risk of being infected with *trichinae* (see Chapter 1). Venison (deer) does not eat meat so it is excluded. Freezing will not kill larval cysts in bears and other wild game animals that live in Northwestern U.S. and Alaska. That meat has to be cooked to 71° C (160° F) internal temperature.

Wild game meat is lean and darker than other meats due to a lot of physical activity the animal is subjected to. This requires an increased supply of oxygen and as a result more myoglobin is developed. The more myoglobin is present the darker the color of the meat. Such a meat is often tougher but is good for sausages as meat for sausages must be ground first which is a tenderizing step. Sausages made of venison are commercially made for sale in Canada and Alaska. Venison is lean meat and it should be mixed with pork back fat, fatty pork or a combination of pork and beef. A proportion of 60% venison to 40% other fatter meats is a good choice. You can add 30% of pork back fat or fat pork trimmings.

Wild Fowl

The meat quality of wild birds is less predictable than farm raised chicken or turkey due to the different age of the birds that reside in different areas. They have fed on an unknown diet which affects the flavor of the meat. What is predictable is that these birds are very lean and will benefit from receiving some pork fat.

The same rules and processing steps apply to wild game as for other sausages. Wild game sausages benefit from using strong spices such as rosemary, smoked paprika, onion or garlic powder, ground celery, thyme, ginger, juniper, sage, parsley, marjoram, and dry mustard. Curry powder imparts a characteristic flavor to food and may be used by those who like this spice.

Chapter 5

Creating Your Own Recipes

Creating Your Own Recipes

It is mind boggling to see people clicking for hours on a computer keyboard to find magic recipes on the Internet. Searching for the Holy Grail of a sausage. Then when they find something they like, they mess it up by applying too high smoking or cooking temperatures. The recipe of course, gets the blame. Then they look for another magic recipe again.

Recipe is what the word says: "the recipe", it does not imply that one will produce an outstanding sausage. Making quality sausages has little to do with recipes, *it is all about the meat science and the rules that govern it.* All sausage making steps, especially temperature control, are like little building blocks that would erect a house. It is like the strength of the chain, which is only as strong as its weakest link.

Each step in sausage making influences the step that follows, and all those steps when performed correctly will, as a final result, create the quality product.

We could fill this book with hundreds of recipes but that won't make you more knowledgeable. *There isn't one standardized recipe for any of the sausages.* The best meat science books written by the foremost experts in this field list different ingredients for the same sausage. Salami Milano and Salami Genoa are basically the same sausage, the difference lies mainly in meat particle size. Replacing mace with nutmeg, using caraway or cumin, or adding white or black pepper will have little effect on a sausage. There are sausages where a dominant spice plays a huge role, for example the Italian fresh sausage must include fennel otherwise it will lose its character.

The same sausage made from the same recipe carries a different name when made in a different country. Take for example traditionally made fermented sausage such as dry salami. In Italy it is called salami, in Spain salchichón, in Hungary salami, in Poland salami, in France Saucisson sec, yet it is made from the same materials with the same processing steps. It will be smoked in Poland and Hungary, in some regions customers expect it to be covered with white mold, but these are minor differences. In Mexico and in southern USA people are fond of hot food and sausages, in Europe much less. Chinese add plenty of sugar to sausages, but when combined with soy sauce such sausage tastes pleasant. The same sausage may be packed into large or small diameter casings, its taste will remain the same. In France a large diameter sausage is called "Saucisson" and the small one "Saucisse". Saucisson de Toulouse is a big sausage and Saucisses de Toulouse a small one, both of course taste the same.

Study reliable recipes to get the feel of the subject and you will notice how similar they are. The same amount of salt and spices, the same smoking and cooking temperatures, and so on. In each case *the underlying technology, processing, temperatures, all these are equal everywhere.* Then comes the moment when you say why do I waste time looking for all those recipes, let me make a good liver today and salami tomorrow. And like a good cook who does not need a chicken soup recipe, you can create sausages without any notes. And from that moment you can quote Madame Benoit, the famous Canadian cookery expert and author who once said:

> *"I feel a recipe is only a theme, which an intelligent cook can play each time with a variation."*

A Little Goes the Long Way

Basically a sausage is meat, salt and pepper. I will never forget when I made my first Polish smoked sausage that turned out very well and I proudly gave it to my friend - professional sausage maker Waldemar to try. I have included the standard ingredients, but I have also added nutmeg and other spices that I liked. Well my friend's judgement was as follows:

> *"Great sausage, but why all those perfumes?"*

For him it was supposed to be the classical Polish Smoked Sausage and all it needed was salt, pepper, marjoram and garlic. The moral of the story is that putting dozens of spices into the meat does not guarantee the best product.

The owner of a popular Texas barbecue restaurant was asked this question: "what do you put inside your sausages that they taste so great?" The answer was: *"it is not what I put into them, but what I don't put is what makes them so good."*

Keep it simple. Combining meat with salt and pepper already makes a great sausage providing that you will follow the basic rules of sausage making. If you don't cure your meats properly, grind warm fat or apply too high smoking and cooking temperatures, all the spices in the world will not save your sausage.

Make Friends with the Metric System

Our discussions are based on the metric system, there is no other way to create recipes in a logical way, so start to use it, after all the whole world does. You are familiar with percents so you already use the metric system.

If you take 100 g of sausage, 1.0% equals 1 g, 1.8% = 1.8 g, 30% = 30 g. You are not going to make such a small amount of sausage, but increasing this amount 10 times will create a more practical sausage to work with. The weight of the sausage now becomes 100 g x 10 = 1000 g which is the same as 1 kg (2.20 lb). Your percents need to also be increased by a factor of 10 as the sausage weighs 1000g; 1% becomes 10 g, 1.8% = 18 g, 30% = 30 g and so on.

Let's say you have 2,400 g (2.4 kg) meat and you want to apply 1% salt. Get the calculator and punch in the numbers: 2400 g x 0.01 (1.0%) = 24 g of salt. You want to add 1.8% salt, the calculation goes the same way: 2400 g x 0.018 (1.8%) = 43.2 g of salt.

The good news is that *there is nothing to calculate if you standardize on making 1000 g (1 kg) of sausage.* Two percent of salt becomes 20 g, 0.2% of pepper becomes 2 g. Calculating liquids is as easy as 1 liter (1000 ml) of water weighs 1 kg (1000 g). Now 30% of water becomes 30 g (or 30 ml), and 5% of water (5 ml) weigh 5 g. Now for the rest of your life you don't need to worry about salt or spices in your recipes.

Professional recipes list ingredients in percents and the total of meat, ingredients and spices comes to 100%. Most professional books list meat or main materials in percents and the total must equal 100%. Then they list all spices together that are needed to make 1 kg of the sausage. If they need 20 kg of the sausage they multiply the spices by a factor of 20.

Note: 1 Tablespoon = 3 teaspoons in both the US and the UK, it holds 15 ml (1/2 fl oz) of water. Australian tablespoon is bigger, it holds 20 ml of water.

The Importance of Salt

The sausage needs salt. Salt is added to flavor the meat and to inhibit growth of bacteria. It also contributes to curing and firmness, water holding and juiciness, binding and texture. In general sausages contain **1.5-2%** salt. Adding more than 3.5% will make a sausage too salty, however, such amount of salt is hardly noticeable in fermented dry sausages.

Fresh sausages. The amount of salt is very flexible and not critical. The salt is added for flavor, it is not needed for safety as the sausage is consumed immediately or within days. About **1.2-1.8%** will work fine. Taste the sausage before stuffing, you can always add more. Refrigerator/freezer takes care of the sausage safety.

Cooked sausages. When the first and the 2nd world wars ended, Europe was severely damaged and suffered from the lack of refrigeration. Sausages needed to last weeks or months at room temperature which in northern Europe was <18°C (<64° F) for half of the year. They were smoked, baked in a smokehouse or cooked in water and then hung in the air where they continued losing moisture becoming dry sausages in time. They were made with **2.0-2.5%** of salt and potassium nitrate and that prevented meat from spoiling as long as the temperature stayed below 18° C (64° F).

Liver sausages and head cheeses. The amount of salt is less critical, it is added for flavor. These are short life sausages that must be kept in a refrigerator. Liver spoils rapidly and head cheese as well due to its large moisture content. Add **1.8%** salt.

Blood sausages. The blood amount can vary from 5% to 100%, the average around 30%. Of course the more blood the shorter the life of the sausage as bacteria thrive on blood. About **1.5-1.8%** of salt will meet the requirement of most blood sausages.

Fermented Sausages. Fermented *dry* sausages need **3.0-3.3% salt** and Cure #2 which contains sodium nitrite and sodium nitrate. Fermented *semi-dry* sausages require **2.5%** salt and Cure #1 which contains sodium nitrite. The amount of salt added to fermented sausages is higher since it provides safety, it protects meat from spoiling.

Fast-fermented spreadable sausages. These are cold smoked, fast made fermented sausages. Since they are not cooked they must be kept under refrigeration. They need **2.5%** salt and Cure #1.

Cold smoked sausages. If not subjected to thermal treatment, these sausages are very similar to fermented dry sausage and require 3% salt and Cure #2.

If you want a consistent product, weigh out your salt. Estimating salt per cups or spoons can be deceiving as not all salts weigh the same per unit volume. Kosher salts are less dense than ordinary table salts and measure quite differently from a volume standpoint. A given weight of Diamond® Crystal takes up nearly twice the volume as the same weight of table salt. One teaspoon of table salt weighs 6 g but 1 teaspoon of Kosher salt weighs 4.8 g.

When using a scale it makes no difference what kind of salt you choose. Ninety grams of table salt equals 90 g of flaked salt regardless of the volume they might occupy. As you can see it is *always advisable to weigh out your salt.*

Sugar. As a flavoring ingredient, sugar plays a little role, although Chinese sausages contain up to **5%** of it. They also include soy sauce and the combination of two is quite satisfying. Adding sugar at more than **3%** is noticeable. Sugar is added to fermented sausages so that friendly bacteria can produce lactic acid which will prevent undesirable bacteria from spoiling the meat. In the past potassium nitrate was used to cure meat and sugar was added to enhance the growth of curing bacteria that forced potassium nitrate into releasing nitrite, which in turn cured the meat. Sugar is listed in some old recipes, however, it was not added to flavor the sausage. Adding **0.1-0.2%** of sugar helps to preserve the color of the sausage. Adding sugar to cold smoked fermented dry sausages will trigger fermentation and may create a sourly flavor. If by mistake too much salt was added to meat, then adding some sugar may help offset the harshness of salt.

Herbs, Spices and Seeds

Many sausages include a dominant spice which gives them a recognized flavor, for example Italian Sausage (fennel), American Breakfast Sausage (sage), Kabanosy (nutmeg, caraway), Polish Smoked Sausage (garlic, marjoram), Hunter's Sausage (jumiper), Curry Sausage (curry). The hotness of the sausage is easily controlled with cayenne pepper.

The spices are applied at around **0.1-0.2%** (1-2 g/kg). Ginger, cardamom and cloves are potent and aromatic and are applied at less than **0.05%** (0.5 g/1 kg). Cayenne pepper is extremely hot so start at less than **0.05%**. Dark spices such as nutmeg, caraway, cloves, and allspice can darken the color of the sausage.

Anise is the star shaped dried fruit of *Pimpinella anisum*. Its flavor resembles that of fennel and of course it is added to fresh *Italian sausage* or sausages such as *Mortadella* or *Pepperoni*.

Allspice. It gets its name because it has flavor similar to the combination of cinnamon, cloves and nutmeg. Allspice can be used in any meat product or sausage. Some examples: *Swedish potato sausage, bologna, hotdog, frankfurter* and *head cheese*.

Bay leaf is principally used in vinegar pickles in products such as pigs feet, and lamb and pork tongues.

Caraway seed is the dried fruit of caraway plant which grows in Europe and the United States. An aromatic seed, somewhat resembling the cumin seed, often added to rye bread, sauerkraut, pickles and some sausages, for example *Kabanosy*.

Cardamom is the fruit that consists of a shell containing the seeds. Cardamom seeds are used in *liver sausages* and *head cheese*.

Celery seeds are used in pork sausages.

Chili peppers - originated in Mexico and spread all over the world. They have white, yellow, red or purple to black fruits and a varying degree of hotness.

Chili powder - a combination of chili pepper, cumin, oregano and garlic

Cinnamon - is the dried bark of *Cinnamomum Casia* tree which grows in India and China. Often added to *blood sausages* and *bologna*.

Clove means nail (clavo) in Spanish and the dried flowers resemble a nail with its sharp point. Cloves go well with *emulsified sausages, head cheese, liver* and *blood sausages.* Cloves are usually inserted into hams which are baked.

Coriander seed is the dried fruit of the cilantro herb. Used in *emulsified sausages, Polish sausages, minced hams* and *pastrami.*

Cumin seed is principally used for making curry powder. It is also added to home made chili.

Curry - is a a combination of spices usually including ground turmeric, cumin, coriander, ginger, and fresh or dried chilies.

Dill seed or leaf is added to vinegar when making cucumber pickles. Very popular in Eastern Europe where it is added to chicken soup or boiled potatoes.

Fennel is the dried seed of the fennel plant. It is added to fresh Italian sausage.

Garlic, after pepper may be considered the most popular ingredient added to sausages. It also comes in dehydrated powder which is preferred as it saves storage and eliminates chores such as peeling and chopping. If using garlic powder use about 1/3 of the weight of fresh garlic. Although the flavor of fresh or granulated garlic is basically the same, fresh garlic has a much stronger aroma which unfortunately dissipates very fast.

Ginger is used in cooked sausages (white head cheese, liver sausage).

Juniper - berries from juniper tree or bush are a spice used in a wide variety of culinary dishes and best known for the primary flavoring in gin. Usually added to wild game sausages and Hunter sausages.

Mace and Nutmeg can leave a bitter taste when more than 0.01% (1g/1 kg of meat) is added. They come from the same large tree that grows in Malaysia. Mace is the covering of the seed (nut). The hard nut becomes nutmeg. As a rule they are not used in fresh sausages as their aroma is easily noticeable. Mace is often used in *liver sausages, frankfurters, hot dogs* and *bologna.*

Marjoram is added to liver sausages, head cheese and many Polish sausages.

Mustard is the seed of the mustard plant which is grown all over the world. There is yellow mustard (most popular), brown mustard and black mustard seed.

Onion is added to liver sausage and other sausages. It also comes in dehydrated powder which is preferred as it saves storage and eliminates chores such as peeling and chopping.

Oregano - popular herb in Italian and Spanish cuisine. Added to chorizos.

Paprika is of two different kinds: Hungarian which is sweet, and Spanish which is slightly pungent. Paprika is a well known colorant and will give the sausage an orange tint. It goes well with *emulsified sausages (hot dog, bologna)* or any pork sausage.

Pepper. Black pepper is normally used in fresh sausages, regular cooked and blood sausages, fermented sausages.

White pepper is commonly used in emulsified and liver sausages. The dividing line is *whether you want to see the pepper in your product or not.* Otherwise it makes no difference and you can replace black pepper with the same amount of white pepper, although black pepper is a bit hotter. Pepper is added at 0.1-0.4% (1.0-4.0 g per 1 kg of meat). The definition of pepper can be confusing at times. Both white and black pepper are produced by the same plant. Black pepper - unripe seeds of the plant with the skin left on. White pepper - ripe seeds with the skin removed.

Pimentón which is Spanish smoked paprika. It comes as sweet, medium or hot variety and is always used in the highest quality *chorizos.*

Quatre épices (4 spices) – a French spice combination that can vary in strength and combination of spices; however, it always contains: nutmeg, cinnamon, and cloves. The fourth ingredient can be ginger, allspice, or caraway or their combination.

Red pepper can be referred to as Cayenne pepper as both are very hot.

Rosemary is a woody, perennial herb with fragrant, evergreen, needle-like leaves. It has a characteristic and strong aroma which goes well with roasted and barbecued meats as well as with wild game meats and sausages. Add at 0.01% (1 g/1 kg).

Sage is used in pork sausages, for example American breakfast sausage.

Savory is good with any sausage.

Tabasco peppers are grown in Louisiana and fermented into Tabasco sauce.

Thyme is added to liver sausage, head cheese, bockwurst and other pork sausages. Thyme is similar to Marjoram but stronger.

Turmeric is the rhizome or underground stem of a ginger-like plant. It is available as a ground, bright yellow fine powder. It is the principal ingredient in curry powder. Turmeric is a natural yellow colorant. It is added to Asian sausages, for example to Balinese *Urutan* dry sausage.

How many grams of spice or ingredient in one flat teaspoon			
Allspice, ground	1.90	Marjoram, dried	0.60
Aniseed	2.10	Marjoram, ground	1.50
Basil	1.50	Milk powder	2.50
Bay leaf, crumbled	0.60	Mustard seed, yellow	3.20
Basil, ground	1.40	Mustard, ground	2.30
Caraway, seed	2.10	Nutmeg, ground	2.03
Cardamom, ground	1.99	Onion powder	2.50
Cayenne pepper, ground	2.50	Oregano, ground	1.50
Celery seed	2.50	Paprika, ground	2.10
Cilantro, dry	1.30	Parsley, dry	0.50
Cinnamon, ground	2.30	Pepper-black, ground	2.10
Cloves, ground	2.10	Pepper-white, ground	2.40
Coriander, ground	2.00	Pepper, flakes, red	2.30
Coriander, seed	1.80	Pepper. whole	4.00
Cumin, ground	2.00	Poppy seed	2.84
Cumin seed	2.10	Rosemary, leaf	1.20
Cure #1 or Cure #2	6.00	Saffron	0.70
Curry powder	2.50	Sage, ground	0.70
Dill, whole	2.42	Savory	1.72
Fennel, whole	2.00	Salt	6.00
Fenugreek, ground	3.70	Soy powder	3.00
Garlic powder	2.80	Sugar	5.00
Ginger, ground	1.80	Tarragon, dry	1.00
Juniper berries	1.53	Thyme, crumbled	0.60
Mace, ground	1.69	Turmeric, ground	3.00

Note: 1 tsp of dried ground spice weighs 2 grams. If using onion powder use about 1/3 of the weight of fresh onion.

Vinegar though not a spice is used in some sausages like *white head cheese* or Mexican *chorizo*.

Cold water added during mixing absorbs extracted proteins and makes the mass sticky. The finer degree of comminution the more water can be absorbed by the meat. This also depends on meat type, for example beef can absorb much more water than pork. Crushed ice or cold water is added when making emulsified products.

Soy protein concentrate/isolate bind water and will make the sausage plumper. Usually added at 1-3%. (1-3g/1kg).

Non-fat dry milk binds water and makes the sausage firmer. Add at 1-3% (1-3g/1 kg)

Egg is often added to sausages to increase binding ingredients. It should be noted that only the egg white possesses binding properties and egg yolk contributes to more fat and calories. Eggs are often added to fresh sausages, but keep in mind that they contribute to premature spoiling of the sausage.

Egg white is often added (1-3%) to frankfurters with low meat content. It increases protein content, forms stable gel and contributes to a firm texture of the sausage. Powdered egg whites are also available and you generally mix 2 teaspoons of powder with 2 tablespoons of water for each white.

Powdered gelatin, added at 1%, helps to bind de-boned meat together or stuffing individual cuts of meat which are not perfectly lean.

Flour and starch. Adding 1-3% of potato flour to minced meat was widely practiced in the past and it offered many advantages. It made sausages cheaper which was important after the II World War ended and it improved the mouthfeel of low fat products. Flour binds water and contributes to a firm texture.

Starch is often added to sausages with low meat content. Starch is added when making sauces, to trap moisture and to make the sauce heavy. In sausages starch is used for its properties to bind water and to improve texture of the product. The most common sources are potato, wheat, corn, rice and tapioca. Many Russian sausages were made with 2% potato starch. You can add as much as you like but around 5% will be the upper limit. Starch is a common additive in extended injected products like a ham. Another advantage is that unlike flour-thickened sauces it doesn't separate when frozen. Starch has the ability to swell and take on water. The swelling of the starch occurs during the heating stage.

In food applications a starch is twice as effective as the flour it was made from. Flour produces yellowish gel, but the gel obtained from starch is clear.

Phosphates are the universally used by commercial producers as they are the most effective water holding agents. Salt and most water binding agents force meat protein to swell which helps them trap and hold more water. Phosphates are able to open the structure of the protein which helps them hold even more water. This increased water holding capacity of the protein is what prevents water losses when smoking and cooking.

Curing accelerators speed up color formation. These substances accelerate the reaction of sodium nitrite with meat's myoglobin resulting in the development of the red color.

Ascorbic acid (vitamin C) - should not be added with sodium nitrite at the same time as they react violently creating fumes. Therefore ascorbic acid should be added last. A vitamin C tablet may be pulverized and applied to meat. It is usually applied at 0.1%.

Ascorbate is added at 0.4-0.6 g per kilogram of total mass, ascorbate or erythorbate are added at 0.5-0.7 g per kilogram of total mass.

MSG (monosodium glutamate) once chiefly associated with foods in Chinese restaurants is a very effective flavor enhancer. It is now found in many common food items, particularly processed foods. Added at 0.3-1.0%.

Creating Your Own Recipe

1. Choose the sausage type you want to make (fresh, smoked, fermented, cooked, uncooked etc). This step will influence the selection of meat, the amount of salt and nitrite (if any) and the processing steps that will follow. In case a specialty sausage such as liver sausage, head cheese or blood sausage is chosen, different meats and fillers will be selected. If you decide on a known sausage, add spices which are typical for this sausage.

2. Weigh in your spices and salt. Decide how much salt you want to add. All you need is a calculator. For example you have 5 kg (11 lb) of meat and you would like to have 1.8% of salt in your sausage.
0.018 x 5000 grams = 90 g = 5 Tbsp = 15 tsp of salt.

Let's say you are on a low sodium diet so you want to use 1.2% salt only.
0.012 x 5000 g = 60 g (3.3 Tbsp)

Salt for 1 kg (2.2 lbs) of meat				
1%	1.2%	1.5%	1.8%	2%
10 g	12 g	15 g	18 g	20 g

3. Choose the amount of Cure #1. You can be flexible with sodium nitrite (Cure #1), too. Although the maximum allowed by law limit for comminuted meats is 156 ppm (parts per million), there is no established lower limit. European limit is 150 ppm. Denmark has won a concession from the European Common Market and their max nitrite limit is only 100 ppm. You want at least 50 ppm for any meaningful curing to take place but whether the amount is 150 ppm, 120 ppm or 100 ppm you will be fine.

U.S. Cure #1 (6.25% sodium nitrite) for 1 kg (2.2 lbs) of meat			
75 ppm	100 ppm	120 ppm	156 ppm - max
1.2 g	1.6 g	1.9 g	2.5 g

European Peklosol (0.6% sodium nitrite) for 1 kg (2.2 lbs) of meat			
75 ppm	100 ppm	120 ppm	150 ppm - max
12.5 g	16.6 g	20 g	25 g

One flat teaspoon holds 6 g of cure.

European Peklosol can be substituted for salt and the nitrite limits would be observed. Adding 20 g Peklosol to 1 kg of ground meat would result in 120 ppm (parts per million) of sodium nitrite and 2% saltiness. Increasing nitrite levels (ppm) higher would result in a salty product, for example adding 25 g of Peklosol results in 150 ppm limit but the percentage of salt becomes 2.5%. American Cure #1 is stronger as it contains 6.25% sodium nitrite. Adding 2.5 g of Cure #1 (½ tsp) to 1 kg of ground meat results in 156 ppm. This corresponds to adding 1 tsp of Cure #1 to 5 pounds of meat. This is still the safe amount and you may make it your standard formula.

For those who like to be perfect it must be noted that adding Cure #1 brings extra salt into the sausage mass as Cure #1 contains 93.75% salt. This amount should be included in salt total. By now you should be aware that you don't need nitrite for sausages which will not be smoked. Nevertheless some products such as head cheese or blood sausage, although not smoked, might incorporate nitrite to cure meats such as tongues in order to develop the red color expected by the consumer. Keep in mind that *nitrite does not cure fat* and if your sausage is on the fat side, *less nitrite will do the job.*

You should not decrease the amount of salt and nitrite when making traditionally fermented sausages. In those sausages salt and nitrite provide the only protection during the initial stages of the process against spoilage and pathogenic bacteria and they should be applied at the maximum allowed limits.

Show Material

Some sausages display solid chunks of meat or fat inside, nuts, whole peppers, yellow cheese, slices of green or red bell peppers or olives. For example Mortadella is often made with pistachio nuts, some sausages contain whole peppers. Soppressata contains large pieces of fat inside. There are sausages with solid chunks of meat inside, for example Polish Krakowska sausage which is known as Krakauer in Germany. After cubes of lean meat are cured in order to develop a solid red color, they are mixed with finely ground or emulsified meat. Solid chunks of white fat look quite striking in a black blood sausage. Liver sausages often include pieces of white fat, sometimes raisins. Such a sausage does not contain more fat than others. Were this fat emulsified with the rest of meat we would not be able to see it, though it would still be inside. French dry sausages are made with hazelnuts, walnuts or camembert cheese. Head cheese, especially meat jellies include a variety of meats imbedded in aspic. Meat jellies are most attractive since they are richly decorated with vegetables, hard boiled eggs and herbs.

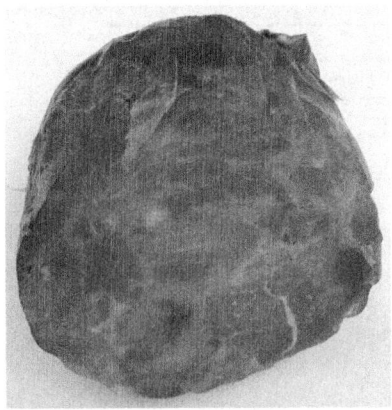

Photo 5.2 Sopressata sausage - fat used as show material.

Photo 5.1 Krakowska sausage - chunks of lean meat used as show material.

Brief summary of important issues for making different type of sausages

Manufacturing process is covered in Chapter 4, here we provide some tips and additional details.

Fresh sausages. Fresh sausages must be fully cooked before serving which can be accomplished by boiling, baking, frying, barbecuing or grilling. They taste best when fried, barbecued or grilled. Do not save on fat, a fresh sausage needs a lot of it otherwise it will have a poor texture after cooking. Italian sausage and bratwurst are good examples.

Cooked and emulsified sausages. These sausages are ready to eat at any time, but taste very good when boiled in water. There is nothing wrong with grilling them, the best example is hot dog or frankfurter. Many cooked sausages contain fillers such as rusk, potatoes, oats, rice, and bread and will not taste good when served cold.

Smoked and cooked sausages. Smoked sausages are best when consumed cold. A lot of time and preparation is involved to produce a quality smoked sausage and it will be a waste to grill it. On the other hand it is recommended to fry or grill a mass produced smoked sausage as it is hardly edible when consumed cold.

People smoke meat, fish, cheese even eggs, but let's be practical. It makes little sense to smoke blood sausage which is filled with rice and onions. To produce an outstanding smoked sausage the meat should be cured. Proper curing needs *time*, extra containers, space and labor and that is something that commercial producers don't have. Instead they use curing solutions and meat tumblers to speed up the process. Hundreds of needles inject a curing solution into the meat which is then inserted into tumblers. Inside the tumbler rotating paddles throw meat pieces around to uniformly distribute the curing solution. The solution consists of salt, sodium nitrite (color development), ascorbic acid (color acceleration), sodium erythorbate (color acceleration) phosphate (binding water), carrageenan (better slicing) and other ingredients, not forgetting a large amount of water.

There is something that curing solution cannot accomplish in such a short time - it cannot develop the *curing flavor* which is present in top quality meats and sausages. A slice of top quality *smoked* ham will emit a pleasant aroma - the ham's natural flavor which was developed by meat reacting with salt and sodium nitrite. A similar aroma is present in top quality Italian or Spanish *dry* hams which are usually not smoked.

So here presents itself an intriguing question: if the best hams develop a beautiful aroma, can a sausage have it as well? It certainly can and in the past all European sausages were made with cured meat. Nowadays everybody seeing pink meat assumes that it was cured, well it was but not long enough to develop the curing flavor. The traditional curing method will develop the curing flavor, the alternative method of curing will only develop the red color. Curing meat for sausages is described in Chapter 1, however, we repeat the paragraph:

Curing procedure

Meat should be cut into smaller pieces, about 2 inches (5-6 cm) and not heavier than 0.5 lb (250 g). Then it is thoroughly mixed with salt and Cure #1, and packed tightly in a container, not higher than 8 inches (20 cm). Then the meat is covered with a clean cloth and stored in a refrigerator. The cloth prevents oxygen in the air from reacting with sodium nitrite which might weaken the process. In addition there are chemical reactions taking place inside the meat and the cloth allows the gases to escape through.

The curing times at 4° C (40° F) (refrigerator temperature) are as follows:

- Meat pieces size 2" - 72 hours.
- Ground meat - 24 - 36 hours, depending on particle size.

Making Fish Sausage

An example of a fish sausage recipe:

Fish flesh 80%, pork fat 8%, wheat starch 8%, salt 2.5%, sugar 1.0%, spices 0.5%

1. Grind skinless and boneless pieces of fish. Different species of fish can be mixed together. Adding pork fat will make a great sausage. Those who object to using pork, can add some vegetable oil (if needed). The flesh of the fish is very soft and it should be partly frozen for the clean cut.
2. Mix ground fish with all ingredients. Adding binders such as flour, cornstarch, bread crumbs or cooked rice, helps to develop a good texture. White of an egg is an excellent binder which is added to many sausages. Fish flesh is very light and white pepper will not be visible. Fish goes well with lemon so adding lemon salt or grated lemon zest is a good idea.
3. Stuff into casings. If you use binders (flour, bread crumbs etc) stuff casings loosely.
4. Smoking (optional).
5. Cook in water at 80° C (176° F) until fish sausage reaches 145° F (63° C) internal temperature. If other meat was added cook to 72° C (160° F) internal temperature.
6. Store in refrigerator.

Fermented Sausages

Choosing the sausage type is the first step as it determines fermentation and drying temperatures, total production time, amount and type of sugar used, type of starter cultures and other factors. *By now you should realize that with one recipe you can make different sausage types (slow or fast-fermented).* Twenty years ago a hobbyist had only one choice, and that was a slow-fermented sausage. Today starter cultures are easily obtainable and all types of fermented sausages can be produced at home. Classical dry fermented sausages are the hardest to manufacture. They also require the most time and care. Therefore it is advised to start with semi-dry sausages first which are faster, easier and safer to produce.

Use of fresh spice in fermented products is generally not a good idea. Fresh spices being moist may contain bacteria, insects, and molds, which will be introduced into the sausage and may affect the process. Spices are very volatile and lose their aroma rapidly and will be largely absent in sausages that take three months to make.

Summary of Important Issues

- Grind only cold or partially frozen meat and fat. Keep it in a refrigerator until ready for mixing.
- When mixing meats by hand, don't just mix but knead the mass with some force. You want to extract proteins which were cut during the grinding/cutting process. You will know when it happens as the mixture will become sticky.
- For better flavor add meat stock or bouillon instead of water when mixing.
- Add fat last when mixing everything together. Scald with hot water fat cubes which will become show material. It prevents fat from being discolored.
- Always taste the sausage mass before stuffing casings as there is still time for corrections. Make a tiny patty, fry it and taste. *A recipe is just a recipe and let your palate be the final judge.*
- Stuff sausages firmly and remove any air pockets with a needle. Blood and liver sausages are stuffed loosely as they are known to expamd.
- Let sausages treated with sodium nitrite rest (conditioning step) for 1-2 hours at room temperature before starting the smoking process or hold them in a smokehouse at 40-50° C (104-122° F) until they feel dry before applying smoke.
- Do not apply smoke when casings are still wet.
- Keep smoke temperature below 72° C (160° F), preferably at 60° C (140° F).
- Do not bake suasages in smokehouse above 85° (185° F). Cool baked sausages in air.
- Cook sausages in water at 80° C (176° F).
- Cool cooked sausage in cold water, then dry in air to evaporate moisture. Cooling prevents shrivelling. Eliminate surface grease from sausages by scalding them with hot water.

United States Department of Agriculture recommends cooking raw to 72° C (160° F), however, you will often notice that some recipes call for 68-70° C (154-158° F). Meats that were treated with salt and sodium nitrite develop some resistance against bacteria and are often cooked to lower temperatures. However, when making sausages for sale stay with the USDA guidelines.

If you make sausage for yourself – add whatever you like, it is your sausage so you might as well like it. If you make sausages for others, well now you have to create a product they will be satisfied with. And don't be afraid to experiment with spices, most people are afraid of them. Read a nutrition label on any food product, it contains spices that agree together so follow the trend.

Salt, pepper and spices are usually applied at certain fixed proportions, of course a regional preference might call for a different amount. What people in Mexico might call a mild sausage, people in Poland or Germany may find unpleasant.

Photo 5.3 Variety of smoked meats and sausages.

Chapter 6

Sausage Recipes

There are hundreds of popular sausages and they cannot be listed in a small book. We have presented 65 recipes of different types of sausages that offer educational value. The purpose of the book is to convince the reader that once he understands the sausage making basics, he can create his own recipes. He can find more than 1,000 sausage recipes for further study at www.meatsandsausages.com

Sausage types: F-fresh, C-cooked, L-liver, B-blood, H-head cheese, FM-fermented

Fresh Sausages

Alheira de Mirandela

In 1497 Jews in Portugal were given the choice of either being expelled from the country or converting to Christianity. In order not to attract the attention of the Portuguese authorities people in the municipality of Mirandela started to make sausages with other meats such as poultry and game which were mixed with bread. The sausages tasted good and in time became popular amongst Christians as well.

Place meats in a skillet and cover with water. Bring to a boil, then simmer until done. Drain meats and save the broth. Slice the bread, place in a bowl and add the broth. When the bread is soft, mash it adding salt and spices. Grind meats through 3/8" (10 mm) plate. Stuff into 32 mm casings, making 8" (20 cm) long links. Smoke with thin cold smoke at 18° C (64° F) for 2 days. Refrigerate. Fry in oil before serving.

Beef	400 g	0.88 lb
Veal	200 g	0.44 lb
Chicken	200 g	0.44 lb
Wheat bread	200 g	0.44 lb

Ingredients per 1 kg (2.2 lb) of material

Salt	18 g	3 tsp
Pepper	2.0 g	1 tsp
Paprika	2.0 g	1 tsp
Cayenne	1.0 g	1 tsp
Garlic, smashed	10 g	3 cloves
Olive oil	45 ml	3 Tbsp

Boudin - Cajun

Boudin is an American Cajun sausage (not to be mistaken with French Boudin Blanc) made with pork meat, rice and pork liver; the liver is a must for a really good sausage. Boudin is the most popular sausage in southwest Louisiana and can be purchased from just about every supermarket, convenience store and restaurant.

Place meat, liver, chopped onion, chopped celery, bay leaf and pepper in 1 quart (950 ml) of water and bring to a boil. Reduce heat and simmer for 1 hour until meat separates from the bone. Remove the meat, discard the vegetables, strain and save the stock. Bring stock to boil and add rice. Simmer until rice is tender. Grind all meat through 1/4" plate. Mix ground meat with chopped green onions, chopped parsley, salt, white pepper, cayenne and rice. Add stock until mixture does not stick to your fingers. Stuff into 32 - 36 mm hog casings. Make 12" (30 cm) links. Boudin is served hot, baked or boiled.

Pork butt	700 g	1.54 lb
Pork liver	300 g	0.66 lb

Ingredients per 1 kg (2.2 lb) of meat

Salt	18 g	1 Tbs
Black pepper, cracked	6.0 g	3 tsp
Dried thyme	2.0 g	1½ tsp
Cayenne pepper	2.0 g	1 tsp
Parsley, fresh	2 Tbsp	2 Tbsp
Onion	60 g	4 Tbs
Green onions (scallions)	30 g	1 stalk
Celery, cut up	30 g	1 rib
Bay leaf, crushed	1/2 leaf	
Rice	150 g	1 cup
Cold water	100 ml	3.3 oz fl

Bratwurst-German

Bratwurst is a German fresh light colored sausage made from uncured meat. The best quality bratwurst is produced from veal and pork, however, the sausages made from all pork are common as they cost less to produce. Depending on the region where the sausage was made and the combination of spices which were added, we may find bratwursts with many names, such as: Thuringer Bratwurst, Nurnberger Bratwurst, Rheinishe Bratwurst and many others.

Pork	700 g	1.54 lb
Veal	300 g	0.66 lb

Ingredients per 1 kg (2.2 lb) of meat

Salt	18 g	3 tsp
White pepper	3.0 g	1.5 tsp
Marjoram, dry	1.0 g	1 tsp
Caraway	1.0 g	1/2 tsp
Nutmeg	1.0 g	1/2 tsp
Ginger, ground	0.5 g	1/2 tsp
White of an egg	2	2
Cold water	100 g	3,3 oz fl

Grind meat through 3/16" plate (5 mm).
Whisk the eggs. Mix meats and all ingredients together.
Stuff into 32-36 mm hog casings forming 4" (10 cm) links.
Keep in refrigerator. Cook before serving.

Note: adding white of an egg is optional. It is common in Germany to add eggs into fresh sausages to increase the binding of ingredients.
Bratwurst sausage is usually fried or grilled.

Beef Sausage - Kosher

A very simple to make sausage without pork.

Beef, lean	700 g	1.54 lb
Beef fat (suet)	200 g	0.44 lb
Potato flour	100 g	0.22 lb

Ingredients per 1 kg (2.2 lb) of material

Onion	30 g	1/2 onion
Salt	18 g	3 tsp
Pepper	2.0 g	1 tsp
Water	200 ml	6.6 fl oz

Cut beef into small pieces. Dice onion finely.
Combine flour with salt and spices, add water and mix together. Add meat and fat and mix again. Grind the sausage mass with 1/8" (3 mm) plate.
Stuff into beef or synthetic casings. Place in refrigerator. Cook before serving.

Breakfast Sausage

This is a very popular American sausage. Served by fast food restaurants, given in the form of sausage links to patients in hospitals, sold at supermarkets. Made like most sausages of pork, salt and pepper with sage being the dominant spice.

Pork, semi-fat (butt)　　　1000 g　2.2 lb

Ingredients per 1 kg (2.2 lb) of meat

Salt	18 g	3 tsp
Pepper	2.0 g	1 tsp
Sage (rubbed)	2.0 g	1 tsp
Nutmeg	0.5 g	1/4 tsp
Ginger	0.5 g	1/4 tsp
Thyme (dried)	1.0 g	1 tsp
Cayenne pepper	0.5 g	1/4 tsp
Cold water	100 g	3.3 oz fl

Grind meat with 1/4" (6 mm) plate.
Mix meat with all ingredients, including water.
Stuff into 22-26 mm sheep or 28-30 mm hog casings. Tie into 4" links.
Cook before serving. Recommended for frying or grilling.

Butifarra

Spanish Butifarra sausage is one of the most important dishes of the Catalan cuisine.

Beef	700 g	1.54 lb
Pork jowls, pork belly	300 g	0.66 lb

Ingredients per 1 kg (2.2 lb) of meat

Salt	18 g	3 tsp
Pepper	1.0 g	1/2 tsp
Garlic powder	1.0 g	1/2 tsp
Cinnamon	0.5 g	1/4 tsp
Cayenne	0.5 g	1/4 tsp
Red wine	60 ml	2 oz fl

Grind beef through 1/4" (5 mm) plate.
Grind pork through 3/8" (10 mm) plate.
Mix/knead beef with salt until sticky. Add wine and spices and remix. Add ground jowls and mix all together.
Stuff into 36 mm hog casings, leave in one coil.
Refrigerate. Cook before serving.

Italian Sausage - Sweet

Italian Sausage is a wonderful sausage for frying or grilling and can be found in every supermarket in the USA. Fried with green bell peppers and onions, it is sold by street vendors everywhere in New York City. Don't connfuse it with cheap poached hot dogs on a bun, Italian sausage is bigger and served on a long subway type roll. It is leaner than other fresh sausages and the US regulations permit no more than 35% fat in the recipe. The dominant spice is fennel, occasionally added together with anise, by adding (or not) cayenne pepper a sweet, medium or hot Italian sausage is produced.

Pork butt   1000 g   2.20 lb

Ingredients per 1 kg (2.2 lb) of meat

Salt	18 g	3 tsp
Black pepper, coarse	2.0 g	1 tsp
Sugar	2.0 g	1/2 tsp
Fennel seed, cracked	3.0 g	2 tsp
Coriander	1.0 g	1/2 tsp
Cumin	1.0 g	1/2 tsp
Cold water	90 ml	3 oz fl

Grind meat with 3/8" (10 mm) plate.
Mix meat with all ingredients, including water.
Stuff into 32 - 36 mm hog casings and tie into 6" (15 cm) links.
Cook before serving. Recommended for frying or grilling.

Notes
For medium hot Italian Sausage add 2 g (1 tsp) cayenne pepper.
For hot Italian Sausage add 4 g (2 tsp) cayenne pepper.
Italian spices such as basil, thyme and oregano are often added.

Merguez

Merguez, the French transliteration of the Arabic word mirqaz, is a spicy, short sausage from North Africa made with lamb or beef and flavored with spices. Spices such as paprika, cayenne or harissa, and a hot chili paste that gives Merguez sausage its red color. Sold by street vendors in Paris, can also be found in London, Belgium and New York.

Lamb	1000 g	2.20 lb

Ingredients per 1 kg (2.2 lb) of meat

Salt	18 g	3 tsp
Pepper	4.0 g	2 tsp
Garlic	7.0 g	2 cloves
Cayenne pepper	2.0 g	1 tsp
Allspice, ground	1.0 g	1/2 tsp
Paprika	4.0 g	2 tsp
Cumin	1.0 g	1/2 tsp
Olive oil	14 g	1 Tbsp

Grind meat through 1/4" (6 mm) plate.
Mix ground meat with all ingredients and olive oil.
Stuff into 24-26 mm sheep casings. Leave as one long rope or make 5" links.
Store in refrigerator.
Cook before serving.

Note: some recipes call for a mixture of lamb and beef.
Merguez owes its red color due to the high amount of paprika.
Many recipes call for Harrisa Paste which is a combination of garlic, cumin, olive oil, hot chili peppers and coriander.

Making Harrisa paste:

1. Place 4 oz of red hot chilies in a bowl and cover with hot water for two hours, then drain.
2. In a blender process 1/4 cup garlic cloves, 1/4 cup ground cumin, 1/2 cup ground coriander, 1/4 cup salt, drained chillies and 1/2 cup olive oil. Add olive oil slowly until a thick paste is produced. For a finer consistency rub paste through a sieve.

You can make a smaller amount of paste: 1 garlic clove crushed and finely chopped, 1/2 Tbs salt, 2 Tbs olive oil, 1 tsp cayenne pepper, 1/2 tsp ground cumin, 1/4 tsp ground coriander. Mix ingredients in a jar and shake well. Cover with a lid.

Salchicha de Ternera (*Veal Sausage*)

Small Spanish fresh sausages made from veal.

Veal	700 g	1.54 lb
Pork belly, fat trimmings	300 g	0.66 lb

Ingredients per 1 kg (2.2 lb) of meat

Salt	18 g	3 tsp
Pepper, white	4.0 g	2 tsp
Nutmeg	0.5 g	1/4 tsp
Water, cold	60 ml	2 oz fl

Grind beef and fat through 10 mm (3/8") plate.
Grind fat through 10 mm (3/8") plate.
Grind beef, adding salt and spices through 3 mm (1/8") plate or emulsify in food processor adding 60 ml of cold water.
Mix emulsified paste with fat.
Stuff into 18 mm sheep casings, forming links 10-12 cm (4-5") long.
Refrigerate. Cook fully before serving.

Spanish Chorizo - Mexicano

Original Spanish chorizo is made from coarsely chopped pork and seasoned with oregano, paprika and garlic. Most South American chorizos are of a fresh type which is fried for breakfast or grilled on a fire. Mexican Chorizo is a fresh sausage made from ground pork and seasoned with chili peppers, garlic and vinegar. It is moister and much hotter than the Spanish chorizo.

Pork butt (shoulder)	1000 g	2.20 lb

Ingredients per 1 kg (2.2 lb) of meat

Salt	18 g	3 tsp
Pepper	2.0 g	1 tsp
Paprika, sweet	4.0 g	2 tsp
Cayenne pepper	2.0 g	1 tsp
Oregano, rubbed	2.0 g	2 tsp
Garlic, smashed	7.0 g	2 cloves
White vinegar	50 ml	1/5 cup
Cold water	50 ml	1/5 cup

Grind meat through 12 mm (1/2") plate.
Mix meat, all ingredients, vinegar and water together.
Stuff into 32-36 mm hog casings and make 8" long links.
Keep in a refrigerator.
Cook before serving.

Notes
Chorizo with eggs is often served for breakfast: mix pieces of chorizo with scrambled eggs.

White Sausage *(Weisswurst)*

White sausages are very popular in Germany, especially in Bavaria.

Pork	500 g	1.10 lb
Veal	300 g	0.66 lb
Back fat	200 g	0.44 lb

Ingredients per 1 kg (2.2 lb) of meat

Salt	18 g	3 tsp
White pepper	3.0 g	1.5 tsp
Ginger, ground	0.5 g	1/4 tsp
Fresh parsley, chopped	10.0 g	1 bunch
Onion powder	6.0 g	2.5 tsp
Mace	0.5 g	1/4 tsp
Grated lemon peel	1/4 lemon	
Egg white	2	2
Whole milk	90 ml	3 oz fluid

Grind meat through 3/16" plate (3 mm).

Beat eggs with a whisk.

Add to the processor ground meats, milk and all ingredients and emulsify.

Stuff into 28-32 mm hog casings forming 4" (10 cm) links.

Keep in a refrigerator or freeze for later.

Cook before serving.

Notes:

Eggs are used to bind everything together.

Instead of whole milk you may use 40 g (1.4 oz) of non-fat dry milk which has good binding properties.

One stalk of chopped scallions or chives may be added.

Grate the outside of the lemon only, not the inner white pith.

Cooked Sausages

Andouille

Andouille is a classical American smoked sausage from Louisiana which is used in meals like gumbo or jambalaya. The regional cooking style known as Cajun employs many hot spices and vegetables and is famous for its original sausages: Andouille, Boudain, Chaurice (local version of Spanish chorizo) or Tasso (smoked butt). Depending on the region, the recipes will vary - some recipes include dry red wine, others bay leaves, allspice, sage, paprika, crushed red peppers, sugar, onion powder, pequin pepper, mace, nutmeg, sage, ancho chili and file powder.

Pork, semi-fat (butt)   1000 g   2.20 lb

Ingredients per 1 kg (2.2 lb) of meat

Salt	16 g	2.5 tsp
Cure #1	2.5 g	1/2 tsp
Cracked black pepper	6.0 g	3 tsp
Chopped garlic	10.0 g	3 cloves
Dried thyme	2.0 g	1.5 tsp
Cayenne pepper	2.0 g	1 tsp
Cold water	100 g	3.3 oz fl

Grind meat with 1/4" (6 mm) plate.

Mix meat with all ingredients, including water.

Stuff into 38-40 mm hog casings. Leave as a rope or make 12" (30 cm) links.

Dry for 1 hour at room temperature or preheat smoker to 130° F (54° C) and hold without smoke for one hour.

Apply hot smoke for 2 hours.

Increase smoker temperature to 185° F (85° C) and bake the sausage until internal temperature of 154° F (68° C) is obtained.

Bockwurst

Bockwurst is German white sausage made of pork and veal (beef). Bockwurst was sold in Berlin and Bavaria already 200 years ago.

Beef (shoulder, neck)	400 g	0.88 lb
Pork shoulder, lean	300 g	0.66 lb
Pork back fat	300 g	0.66 lb

Ingredients per 1 kg (2.2 lb) of meat

Salt	18 g	1 Tbs
Cure #1	2.0 g	1/3 ts
White pepper	3.0 g	1½ tsp
Ginger, ground	0.3 g	1/8 tsp
Nutmeg	1.0 g	1/2 tsp
Mace	0.5 g	1/4 tsp
Cold water	100 ml	3.33 oz fl

Separately grind beef, pork and fat through 3/16" plate (3 mm).
Place ground beef in food processor, add Cure #1, salt, cold water and emulsify.
Add pork and spices and emulsify. Lastly add fat and emulsify all together.
Stuff into 28-32 mm hog casings, forming 6" (15 cm) links.
Apply smoke at 60° C (140° F) for 60 minutes.
Cook in water at 80° C (176° F) for 20 minutes.
Cool in water, then dry in air.
Keep in refrigerator.

Boudin Blanc

This is a simple basic French Boudin Blanc.

Pork belly, no rind	550 g	1.21 lb
Full milk	300 ml	0.66 lb
Onions	150 g	0.33 lb

Ingredients per 1 kg (2.2 lb) of material

Butter	28 g	1 oz
Salt	15 g	2.5 tsp
White pepper	2.0 g	1 tsp

Finely chop onions and briefly fry in butter until glassy and without color.
Cut pork belly into 2" (50 mm) pieces. Place in a freezer for 30 minutes. Grind pork belly with onions through 1/4" (5 mm) plate. Refreeze partially and grind again.
Mix ground meat with salt and pepper. Stir in the milk until the sausage paste is quite soft, almost runny. Stuff into 36 mm hog casings making 6" (15 cm) long links. Cook in water at 80° C (176° F) for 35 minutes. Cool in cold water, dry and refrigerate.

Note: for a richer flavor instead of milk you can use cream mixed with a beaten white of egg. To serve, fry in butter or barbecue. You can enhance the flavor by adding 2.g (1 tsp) of "quatre épices" spice mix (nutmeg, ginger, cinnamon, cloves).

Boudin Blanc de Liège

A famous speciality of Liège, Belgian Bratwurst type of a white sausage

Pork shoulder	150 g	0.33 lb
Pork belly	300 g	0.66 lb
White bread	300 g	0.66 lb
Onions	200 g	0.44 lb
Cream	30 ml	1 oz fl
Milk	30 ml	1 oz fl

Ingredients per 1 kg (2.2 lb) of material

Salt	15 g	2-1/2 tsp
White pepper	2.0 g	1 tsp
Nutmeg	1.0 g	1/2 tsp
Cinnamon	0.5 g	1/4 tsp
Cloves, ground	0.3 g	1/8 tsp
Marjoram	1.0 g	1/2 tsp
Egg	2	2

Crumble the bread and mix with cream and milk.
Chop the onions finely and fry at low heat in lard or oil until glassy and golden.
Grind pork shoulder meat and belly through 1/4" (6 mm) plate.
Mix everything together. Stuff into 36 mm hog casings. Cook in hot water at 80° C (176° F) for 35 minutes. Cool in cold water, dry briefly and refrigerate.

Boudin Blanc de Paris

Boudin blanc from Paris.

Pork back fat, fat trimmings, fat trimmings, pork belly	300 g	0.66 lb
Chicken breast	350 g	0.77 lb
Full milk	250 ml	1 cup
Onions	100 g	3.5 oz

Ingredients per 1 kg (2.2 lb) of material

Salt	12 g	2 tsp
Pepper, white	2.0 g	1 tsp
Thyme, rubbed	1.0 g	1 tsp
Allspice, ground	0.3 g	1/8 tsp
Nutmeg	0.5 g	1/4 tsp
Ginger	0.5 g	1/4 tsp
Cloves, ground	0.3 g	1/8 tsp
Egg whites	4	4
Butter	28 g	1 oz

Finely chop onions and briefly fry in butter until glassy and golden. Cool.

Grind chicken with onions through 1/8" (3 mm) plate.

Grind fat through 1/8" (3 mm) plate. Refreeze partially, then grind again.

Mix ground meat and fat with salt and all spices. Stir in the milk and beaten egg whites until the sausage paste is quite soft, almost runny.

Stuff into 36 mm hog casings making 6" (15 cm) long links.

Cook in water at 80° C (176° F) for 35 minutes.

Cool in cold water, dry and refrigerate. To serve, fry in butter or barbecue.

Currywurst

Currywurst is the best selling sausage in Germany. Currywurst sausage is to Germans what hot dog is to Americans. In Berlin, currywurst is served with "curry ketchup." Currywurst is all about the sauce and not the sausage. This means that one can choose bratwurst, bockwurst, frankfurter or any sausage, and as long as it is served with "curry flavored ketchup" it qualifies to be called Currywurst. As they are different types of curry and different types of the sauce produced, considerable variations occur between sausages. Currywurst is consumed everywhere: in Berlin, Hamburg and the industrial Ruhr Area, it is sold by street cart vendors, small restaurants, train stations or served at home. Ready to use curry ketchups and sauces are sold in supermarkets. Currywurst is usually served with a roll, bread or french fries. The simplest preparation of currywurst sauce is to mix curry powder with tomato ketchup according to your own liking. Then sauce is poured over grilled sausage, which is usually sliced into smaller pieces.

Sausage: bratwurst, bockwurst, frankfurter, Italian sausage ....1000 g 2.20 lb

Curry sauce:

Salt	3 g	1/2 tsp	Onion powder may be substituted with 1 medium size onion (60 g). Fry the onion in 2 table spoons (28 g) of vegetable oil until glassy looking, then simmer with tomato sauce and other ingredients. Red vinegar may be added at (1/4 cup, 60 ml)
Curry powder	15 g	2 Tbsp	
Sugar	18.0 g	3 Tbsp	
Pepper	4.0 g	2 tsp	
Paprika	2 g	1 tsp	
Tomato sauce	850 g	30 oz	
Worcestershire sauce	15 ml	1 Tbsp	
Onion powder	2.5 g	1 tsp	

Pour tomato sauce into a preheated skillet. Add all ingredients and mix together. Bring to a boil, reduce heat and simmer for 5 minutes. Fry/broil/grill sausage on each side until brown and cooked. Slice the sausage partially every 1/2 inch. Pour curry sauce over hot sausage. Serve with bread roll.

Note: The invention of currywurst is attributed to Herta Heuwer in Berlin in 1949 after she obtained ketchup, Worcestershire sauce and curry powder from British soldiers. She mixed these ingredients with spices and poured it over grilled pork sausage. Heuwer started selling the cheap but filling snack at a street stand in the Charlottenburg district where it became popular with construction workers rebuilding the devastated city. She patented her sauce, called Chillup, in 1951. At its height the stand was selling 10,000 servings per week. She later opened a small restaurant which operated until 1974.

The demand for ready to use currywurst sauce in Germany is so great that Heinz Company makes ready to use Currywurst Flavored Ketchup, and Knorr Company makes ready to mix with water Currywurst Sauce. Those products can be obtained in the USA online as well.

You can add some Latin flavor to the sausage by adding cilantro, garlic, lemon juice and some cayenne pepper.

Butifarra Blanca *(White Sausage)*

Butifarra is a name for a sausage that originates near Barcelona, in the Catalonia region of Spain. There are versions with rice, in many cases whole eggs are included.

Pork lean, butt	700 g	1.54 lb
Dewlap, jowls	100 g	0.22 lb
Pork belly	200 g	0.44 lb

Ingredients per 1 kg (2.2 lb) of meat

Salt	18 g	3 tsp
White pepper	2.0 g	1 tsp
Cinnamon	1.0 g	1/2 tsp
Nutmeg	0.5 g	1/4 tsp

Grind meats through 1/4" (6 mm) plate.
Mix ground meat with all ingredients.
Stuff into into 36 mm hog casings.
Cook in water at 80° C (176° F) for 35 minutes.
Cool the sausages in cold water.
Drain and place on a table to evaporate the moisture.
Refrigerate.

Butifarra de Huevos *(Sausage with Eggs)*

A simple to make Spanish white sausage with eggs.

Pork lean, ham part	700 g	1.54 lb
Devlap, jowls	100 g	0.22 lb
Back fat or		
hard fat trimmings	200 g	0.44 lb

Ingredients per 1 kg (2.2 lb) of meat

Salt	18 g	3 tsp
White pepper	2.0 g	1 tsp
Eggs, whole	2	2

Grind meats through 1/4" (6 mm) plate.
Mix ground meat with all ingredients.
Stuff into into 36 mm hog casings.
Cook in water at 80° C (176° F) for 35 minutes.
Cool the sausages in cold water.
Drain, briefly dry and refrigerate.

Chicken Sausage-Smoked

All chicken smoked sausage.

Ckicken breast	400 g	0.88 lb
Chicken leg	400 g	0.88 lb
Chicken fat and skin	200 g	0.44 lb

Ingredients per 1 kg (2.2 lb) of meat

Salt	18 g	3 tsp
Cure #1	2.5 g	1/2 tsp
White pepper	2.0 g	1 tsp
Paprika, sweet	2.0 g	1 tsp
Garlic, minced	3.5 g	1 clove
Potato starch	15 g	1 Tbsp
Cold water	30 ml	1 oz fl

Grind meat through 1/4"(6 mm) plate. Mix with salt and cure #1.

Grind skins and fat through 1/8" (3 mm) plate. Place for 30 minutes in a freezer, then grind again.

Mix all ingredients with potato starch and water creating a paste.

Mix ground meat, skin and fat, and the paste together.

Stuff into 36 mm cellulose or fibrous synthetic casings.

Hold for 30 minutes at room temperature.

Smoke at 60° C (140° F) for 60 minutes.

Cook in water at 80° C (176° F) for 35 minutes.

Place in cold water for 10 minutes. Dry briefly and refrigerate.

Chinese Sausage

Chinese sausage is a dried, hard sausage usually made from fatty pork. The Chinese name for sausages is "Lap Chong" which means "winter stuffed intestine" or "waxed intestine" because "chong" not only means "intestine" but also "sausage". This sausage is normally smoked, sweetened, and seasoned. It is used as an ingredient in many dishes in some parts of southern China, including Hong Kong and countries in Southeast Asia. For example, it is used in fried rice, noodle and other dishes. Chinese sausage formulations are unique, based on long traditions.

Ingredients like monosodium glutamate, soy sauce and sugar are added to the sausages in very high levels. The addition of selected Chinese rice wines or even scotch or sherry are common for certain quality products. The most popular spice is cinnamon since Chinese manufacturers believe that it acts as a preservative.

Pork	1000 g	2.20 lb

Ingredients per 1 kg (2.2 lb) of meat

Soy sauce	30 g	1 oz fl
Cure #1	2.5 g	1/2 tsp
Sugar	50 g	4 Tbsp
Monosodium glutamate (MSG)	3.0 g	1/2 tsp
Cinnamon	1.0 g	1/2 tsp
Rice wine	30 ml	2 Tbs
Pepper	2.0 g	1 tsp
Garlic	3.5 g	1 clove
Cold water	60 ml	1/4 cup

Grind pork through 3/8" (10 mm) plate.
Mix ground meat with all ingredients.
Stuff into small diameter hog or sheep casings and make 5" - 6" long links. Tie both ends with a light butcher twine.
Hang sausages at room temperature for one hour.
Apply hot smoke for 45 min.
Bake for about 30 min at 80-85° C (176-185° F) until sausages reach 68-71° C (154-160° F)
Cool in air and refrigerate.

Note: traditional Chinese method of tying sausage casings uses pieces of straw. This is the same technique as the Polish method of using wooden picks which is known as *floking*.

Cotechino Modena

Cotechino is made from leftover trimmings and it always contains a good amount of skin. The word "cotechino" comes from Italian "cotenna" which is the pork rind (skin). The area of production includes the territory of the following Regions in Italy: Emilia-Romagna, Piedmont, Lombardy, Veneto, Marche, Tuscany and Latium, as well as the autonomous Region of Trento.

Pork shoulder, leg meat, belly, jowls, snout	750 g	1.65 lb
Pork skin	250 g	0.55 lb

Ingredients per 1 kg (2.2 lb) of meat

Salt	18 g	3 tsp
Pepper	4.0 g	2 tsp
Nutmeg	0.5 g	1/4 tsp
Cinnamon	0.5 g	1/4 tsp
Cloves, ground	0.3 g	1/8 tsp
Garlic, minced	7.0 g	2 cloves
Cayenne	0.5 g	1/4 tsp

Cook skins in water at 95° C (203° F) until soft. Cool.
Grind lean pork through 3/8" (10 mm) plate.
Grind jowls through 1/4" (5 mm) plate.
Grind skins through 1/8" (3 mm), then
grind again through 1/8" (3 mm) plate *OR*
emulsify in food processor adding 15 ml (1 tablespoon) of cold water.
Mix ground meats with salt until sticky. Add spices, ground jowls and ground/emulsified skins and mix all together.
Stuff into 50-60 mm casings forming 8" (20 cm) long links.
Immerse sausages in hot water and cook at 80° C (176° F) for 60 minutes.
Store in refrigerator.

Notes: although cooked Cotechino is ready to eat at any time, most people heat sausage for about 20 minutes in hot water as it tastes better. Cotechino is often served with lentils or cannellini beans with a sauce alongside mashed potatoes.

Cotechino Modena carries PGI, 1999 classification.

Fish Sausage - Smoked

A basic fish sausage. Fillets of any fish are suitable, however, the sausage will be of better quality when pork fat is included.

Fish fillet	750 g	1.65 lb
Pork belly, back fat		
or fat trimmings	250 g	0.55 lb

Ingredients per 1 kg (2.2 lb) of meat

Salt	15 g	2.5 tsp
Cure #1	2.5 g	1/2 tsp
White pepper	2.0 g	1 tsp
Paprika, sweet	2.0 g	1 tsp
Potato flour	10 g	2 tsp
Lemon peel, grated	1/2 lemon	

Grind fish and pork through 1/8" (3 mm) plate.
Mix with all ingredients.
Stuff into 32 mm hog casings.
Hold for 30 minutes at room temperature.
Smoke at 60° C (140° F) for 60 minutes.
Cook in water at 80° C (176° F) for 30 minutes.
Cool in cold water for 10 minutes, dry briefly and refrigerate.

Frankfurter

German sausages. Frankfurter is similar to bologna sausage, the main difference is the thickness and spice combination. Two parts beef and one part pork is a typical combination. Replacing beef with veal produces the highest quality sausage.

Beef trimmings	700 g	1.54 lb
Pork trimmings	200 g	0.44 lb
Pork back fat or		
hard fat trimmings	100 g	0.22 lb

Ingredients per 1 kg (2.2 lb) of meat

Salt	18 g	3 tsp
Cure #1	2.5 g	1/2 tsp
White pepper	2.0 g	1 tsp
Coriander	1.0 g	1 tsp
Paprika, sweet	1.0 g	1 tsp
Nutmeg	0.5 g	1/4 tsp
Garlic	3.0 g	1 clove
Cold water	240 ml	1 cup

Grind beef through 3/8" (10 mm) plate.
Grind pork through 3/8" (10 mm) plate.
Grind fat through 3/8" (10 mm) plate.
Place ground beef in food processor and emulsify with cold water. Add ground pork, salt, cure #1 and spices and emulsify. Add ground fat and emulsify.
Stuff into 26 mm sheep casings..
Hang in 4° C (38° F) overnight or for 1 hour at room temperature.
Apply smoke at 46° C (115° F) for 1 hour.
Cook in water at around 72° C (160° F) for 30 min until sausages reach 68-70° C (154-158° F) inside .
Place sausages for 5 min in cold water, cool in air and refrigerate.

Glamorgan Sausage

Glamorgan sausage, a traditional Welsh *vegetarian* sausage, made of cheese, leeks and bread crumbs. The sausage is not stuffed into casings, but rather rolled in a cylindrical shape, dipped in egg and coated with bread crumbs.

Bread crumbs	350 g	0.77 oz
Caerphilly cheese, grated	200 g	0.44 oz
Leeks, chopped	250 g	0.55 oz
Eggs	150 g	0.33 oz
Milk	60 ml	2 oz fl

Ingredients per 1 kg (2.2 lb) of material

Salt	12 g	2 tsp
Pepper	2.0 g	1 tsp
Fresh parsley, chopped	5.0 g	1 Tbsp
Thyme or rosemary, dried	2.0 g	1 tsp
Mustard, ground	1.0 g	1/2 tsp
Oil for frying, as needed		

Place the breadcrumbs, cheese, seasoning, mustard, leek and parsley into a mixing bowl, mix well. Beat the eggs and add to the mixture. Add enough milk for the mixture to bind. Divide the mixture into equal parts. Using hands form each portion into a sausage shape.

Coating mix:
Beat another egg and add the milk. Spread the breadcrumbs (or flour) on a plate. Roll each sausage in the egg mixture, then roll in the bread crumbs.
Fry the sausages in oil or melted butter for 5-10 minutes until they become gold-brown. Some people prefer to grill them till golden or bake them in an oven for about 15-20 minutes.

Note: it might be hard finding Caerphilly cheese outside the UK. It is a hard, white, sharp, crumbly cheese with slightly sour tang. You can substitute a mild cheddar-style cheese or feta.

Hurka

Hurka is a well known Hungarian sausage made originally from organ meats such as pork liver, lungs, head meat, rice and onions. Blood is sometimes added.

Pork liver	300 g	0.66 lb
Pork butt	700 g	1.54 lb

Ingredients per 1 kg (2.2 lb) of meat

Salt	12 g	2 tsp
Pepper	2.5 g	1 tsp
Garlic	3.5 g	1 clove
Onion	30 g	2 Tbsp
Cooked rice	150 g	1 cup
Cold water	120 ml	4 oz fl

Boil all meats (except liver) for about 2 hours. Poach liver in hot water until no traces of blood are visible.

Grind meats through 1/4" plate (6 mm).

Grind liver through a 3/16" (3 mm) plate.

Cook rice for about 15 minutes. Place some bacon fat or lard on a frying pan and fry onions until light brown.

Mix everything together, adding 125 ml (½ cup) water. You may substitute some water with white wine.

Stuff loosely into 36 mm hog or synthetic casings.

Cook in water at 85° C (185° F) for 30 minutes.

Note:

Frozen Hurka sausage can be baked at 180° C (350° F) for about 50 minutes (leave the lid on or cover with aluminum foil). Then uncover the sausage and continue baking for 5 more minutes until brown. Fresh Hurka sausage can be pan fried or grilled. Goes well with pickles. Hurka was originally made with 30% pork liver, 30% pork tongues and 10% pork back fat, belly or lard.

Jadgwurst

German Hunter's sausage.

Pork, lean	500 g	1.10 lb
Pork belly	500 g	1.10 lb

Ingredients per 1 kg (2.2 lb) of meat

Salt	18 g	3 tsp
Cure #1	2.5 g	1/2 tsp
Pepper	1.0 g	1/2 tsp
Coriander	1.0 g	1/2 tsp
Mace	0.5 g	1/4 tsp
Mustard, ground	2.0 g	1 tsp
Ginger, ground	0.5 g	1/4 tsp

Grind all meat through 3/8" (10 mm) plate.

Mix meat with all ingredients.

Stuff into 50 mm fibrous casings.

Hang for 30 min at room temperature.

Place sausages for 60 min in pre-heated to 54° C (130° F) smokehouse.

Apply hot smoke for 30 minutes.

Increase smokehouse temperature (no smoke applied) to 76° C (170° F) and cook sausages to 68° C (154° F) internal temperature. Cool in air and refrigerate.

OR

cook in water at 167-172° F (75-78° C) for about 1 hour. Cool sausages in cold water and dry briefly.

Refrigerate.

Kabanosy
(Kabanosy)

The most popular Polish sausage and most likely the finest meat stick in the world. The name Kabanosy comes from the nickname "kabanek" given to a young fat pig no more than 120 kg in weight that was fed mainly potatoes in XIX Poland and in former Polish territories known today as Lithuania (Litwa before).

| Pork, lean | 400 g | 0.88 lb |
| Pork, semi-fat | 600 g | 1.32 lb |

Ingredients per 1 kg (2.2 lb.) of meat

Salt	18 g	3 tsp
Cure # 1	2.5 g	1/2 tsp
Pepper	2.0 g	1 tsp
Nutmeg	1.0 g	1/2 tsp
Sugar	1.0 g	1/5 tsp
Caraway	1.0 g	1/2 tsp

Grind lean pork through 3/8" (8 mm) plate and semi-fat pork through 1/4" (5 mm) grinder plate.

Mix ground pork with all ingredients until sticky.

Stuff into 22 -26 mm sheep casings, forming 60-70 cm (23-27") links. Leave sausage links in a continuous coil.

Hang for 12 hours in a cooler at 2-6°C (35-43°F) *OR* for 30-60 minutes at room temperature.

Apply hot smoke 104-122° F (40-50° C) for 50-60 min. Start increasing the temperature and bake at 85-90° C (185-190° F) for about 20 min at 140-190° F (60-90° C) until the meat reaches 154-160° F (68-71° C) internal temperature. The color of the casings should be dark brown.

Total smoking and cooking time about 70-90 min. Shower with cold water, separate into links and keep refrigerated.

Note: the sausage will not spoil in refrigerator. It will keep losing moisture and will become a dry meat stick.

Krakowska Sausage
(Kiełbasa krakowska)

This sausage has always been one of the top sellers in Poland. The name relates to the city of Krakow, one of the oldest cities in Europe. If you follow the recipe you will see that the sliced sausage contains visible chunks of meat. This popular sausage is made in different forms: dry sausage, semi-dry sausage or a regular hot smoked type.

Pork, lean	450 g	0.99 lb
Pork, semi-fat	350 g	0.77 lb
Pork trimmings rich in connective tissue	100 g	0.22 lb
Beef, lean or semi-fat ..	100 g	0.22 lb

Ingredients per 1 kg (2.2 lb.) of meat

Salt	18 g	3 tsp
Cure # 1	2.5 g	1/2 tsp
White pepper	2.0 g	1 tsp
Coriander	0.5 g	1/4 tsp
Garlic	2.5 g	1 clove

Curing meat. Keep different type of meat separately.

Cut lean pork into 2" (50 mm) chunks. Cut other types into 1" (25 mm) size. Place meats in separate containers and proportionally mix with salt and cure #1.

Pack meat tightly in a container, cover with cloth and place for 3 days in refrigerator. Leave lean pork cubes intact.

Grind semi-fat pork through 3/4" (20 mm) plate.`

Grind pork trimmings and beef through 1/8" (3 mm) plate.

Using food processor emulsify pork trimmings and beef adding 40-50% (90 ml, 3 oz fl) crushed ice or cold water. Add spices during this step.

Mix/knead lean cubes of pork and semi-fat ground pork until sticky. Add emulsified meat and mix all together.

Stuff into 75 mm synthetic fibrous casings. Form 40-45 cm (16-18") links and tie up both ends. Made at one end loop for hanging. Hang for 2-4 hours in a drafty area.

Apply hot smoke 45-60° C (113-140° F) for 110-130 minutes.

Cook in water at 72-75° C (161-167° F) for 55-75 min until meat reaches 68-70° C (154-158° F) internal temperature.

Immerse (or shower) in cold water to cool sausages to 12° C (53° F) or lower. Keep refrigerated.

Mortadella di Bologna

Italian mortadella. The name mortadella originates from the Latin words myrtle (mirtatum) and mortar (mortario) and the sausage was pounded the same way in Italy for hundreds of years. This is not an American pre-packaged and sliced bologna product. It is an emulsified sausage with cubes of white fat, whole peppercorns and pistachio nuts. This sausage is the pride of the city of Bologna, however, it may be produced as Mortadella Bologna in the following Italian regions or provinces: Emilia-Romagna, Piedmont, Lombardy, Veneto, Trento, Marche, Lazio and Tuscany.

Pork	650 g	1.43 lb
Jowls, belly or		
fat trimmings	200 g	0.44 lb
Back fat	150 g	0.33 lb

Ingredients per 1 kg (2.2 lb) of meat

Salt	18 g	3 tsp
Cure #1	2.5 g	1/2 tsp
White pepper	2.0 g	1 tsp
Whole peppercorns	4.0 g	1 tsp
Sugar	5.0 g	1 tsp
Coriander	0.5 g	1/4 tsp
Garlic powder	1.5 g	1/2 tsp
Anise	1.0 g	1/2 tsp
Mace	1.0 g	1/2 tsp
Caraway, ground	0.5 g	1/4 tsp
Pistachios, whole	35 g	1.23 oz
Red wine	60 ml	2 oz fl

Dice back fat into ¼" (6 mm) cubes for use as show meat.

Grind all meats through ¼" (6 mm) plate, refreeze and grind again through ⅛" (3 mm) plate.

Using food processor emulsify ground meats with wine and all ingredients (except whole peppercorns, pistachios and diced fat cubes).

Mix emulsified meat with cubed fat, pistachios and whole peppercorns.

Stuff into large diameter beef casings.

Cook sausages in water at 80° C (176 °F) until meat reaches 67-70° C (152 - 158°F) internal temperature.

Cool and refrigerate.

Note: Mortadella Bologna carries PGI, 1998 European certificate of origin.

Polish Sausage-Hot Smoked
(Polska kiełbasa wędzona)

Polish Hot Smoked Sausage consists of pork, salt, pepper, garlic and optional marjoram. The same ingredients are used for Polish Cold Smoked Sausage; what is different is the manufacturing process. Unfortunately, for marketing purposes most producers call *any ring shaped sausage stuffed into 36 mm casings* Polish Smoked Sausage with a total disregard for the materials and ingredients that go inside.

Pork, lean	400 g	0.88 lb
Pork, semi-fat	600 g	1.32 lb

Ingredients per 1 kg (2.2 lb) of meat

Salt	18 g	3 tsp
Cure #1	2.5 g	1/2 tsp
Sugar	2.5 g	1/2 tsp
Pepper	2.0 g	1 tsp
Marjoram, dry	1.0 g	1 tsp
Garlic	3.5 g	1 clove
Cold water	100 ml	3.3 oz fl

Grind lean pork with a 3/8" (10 mm) plate.

Grind semi-fat pork with 3/16" (5 mm) plate.

Mix spices with cold water.

Mix/knead lean pork adding salt and cure #1 until sticky. Add semi-fat pork and mix all together.

Stuff into 32-36 mm hog casings and form 12-13" (30-35 cm) links.

Hang for 1 hour at room temperature. Place sausages in a preheated to 54° C (130° F) smoker with draft dampers fully open.

When casings feel dry or slightly tacky to the touch apply heavy smoke and keep draft dampers 1/4 open. Smoke for 60-90 minutes.

Cook in water at 80° C (176° F) until meaat reaches 68-71° C (154-160° F) internal temperature.

Shower with water or immerse sausages in cold water and cool to 12° C (53° F). Dry briefly and refrigerate.

Potatiskorv

Potatiskorv is a Swedish potato sausage which is also known as Värmland sausage.

Pork	350 g	0.77 lb
Beef	350 g	0.77 lb
Potatoes, boiled	300 g	0.66 lb

Ingredients per 1 kg (2.2 lb) of material

Salt	18 g	3 tsp
White pepper	6.0 g	3 tsp
Allspice, ground	2.0 g	1 tsp
Onion, chopped	30 g	2 Tbsp
Cold water	60 ml	2 oz fl

Boil the potatoes. Drain.
Grind meats, potatoes and onions through 3/8" (10 mm) plate.
Mix meat with salt, pepper and spices until sticky. Add potatoes and mix again.
Stuff into 36 mm hog casings.
Cook in water at 80° C (176° F) for 35 minutes.
Cool in cold water, dry in air and refrigerate.

Venison Sausage

A deer meat also known as venison is suitable for making sausages. It is very lean meat so it benefits from added pork fat.

Deer meat	650 g	1.43 lb
Pork belly	350 g	0.77 lb

Ingredients per 1 kg (2.2 lb) of material

Salt	18 g	3 tsp
Cure #1	2.5 g	1/2 tsp
Pepper	2.0 g	1 tsp
Garlic, minced	10 g	3 cloves
Marjoram, ground	2.0 g	1 tsp
Mustard seed, ground	2.0 g	1 tsp
Juniper seed, ground	0.5 g	1/4 tsp
Rosemary, ground	0.5 g	1/4 tsp
Water	30 ml	1 oz fl

Grind deer and pork belly with salt and cure #1 through 3/8" (8 mm) plate.
Mix meat, belly fat and all ingredients together.
Stuff into 36 mm hog casings.
Hold for 60 minutes at room temperature.
Smoke at 60° C (140° F) for 120 minutes.
Cook in water at 80° C (176° F) for 35 minutes.
Cool in cold water for 10 minutes, dry briefly and refrigerate.

Liver Sausages

Aachener Weihnachtsleberwurst

Aachener Weihnachtsleberwurst (Weihnachts-*Christmas)* is German Christmas liver sausage that have been produced in the city of Aachener since the 19th century.

Lean pork	300 g	0.66 lb
Pork belly	400 g	0.88 lb
Liver	300 g	0.66 lb

Ingredients per 1 kg (2.2 lb) of meat

Salt	12 g	2 tsp
Cure #1	2.5 g	1/2 tsp
White pepper	1.0 g	1/2 tsp
Coriander	1.0 g	1/2 tsp
Cardamom	0.3 g	1/8 tsp
Ginger	0.3 g	1/8 tsp
Anise, ground	0.5 g	1/4 tsp
Vanilla	3 ml	1/2 tsp
Cream	60 ml	2 oz fl
Onion	50 g	1/2 onion
Cranberries, dried	28 g	1 oz

Immerse liver for 5 minutes in hot water (below the boiling point). Cook meats at 95° C (203° F) until done. Save meat stock. Add any solid remaining cooked fat to the sausage.

Grind lean pork and belly with salt and cure #1 through 1/4" (6 mm) plate.

Dice the onion and fry in lard until glassy.

Grind liver through 1/8" (3 mm) plate.

Using food processor emulsify liver until a smooth paste is obtained. Add cream, spices, onion, ground meat and emulsify all together.

Stuff into 40-60 mm natural or synthetic casings.

Cook in water or the remaining meat stock at 78-80° C (174-176° F). Allow 10 minutes cooking time per 10 mm (1 cm) of the sausage diameter (40 mm casing needs 40 minutes cooking time). Cool for 10 minutes in cold water than finish cooling in air.

The sausage may be smoked for a few hours with cold smoke at 18° C (64° F). In such a case use natural or permeable casings (cellulose, fibrous) that will permit the smoke to go through.

The sausage often includes material such as nuts, apple slices, raisins and cranberries.

Note: Aachener Weihnachtsleberwurst carries PGI, 2016 classification.

Braunschweiger Liver Sausage

German liver sausage.

Pork liver	500 g	1.10 lb
Pork jowls, belly or		
fat pork trimmings	500 g	1.10 lb

Ingredients per 1 kg (2.2 lb) of meat

Salt	18 g	3 tsp
Pepper	2.0 g	1 tsp
Marjoram	2.0 g	1 tsp
Nutmeg	1.0 g	1/2 tsp
Onion	60 g	1 small onion

Cut back fat into 1/4" (6 mm) pieces.

Soak liver in cold running water for 1 hour, remove sinews, cut into slices and cover with water of 90° C (194° F). Poach liver 8-10 min stirring frequently. Cool liver in cold water for about 5 min and leave to drain water away.

Grind liver through 1/8" (3 mm) plate and emulsify in food processor. Grind fat pieces through 1/8" (3 mm) plate and emulsify.

Add salt, spices, onions and mix everything together.

Stuff loosely into pork bungs, pork middles or 65 mm synthetic cellulose casings. Tie the ends with twine and make a hanging loop.

Immerse sausages in boiling water and poach at 80° C (176° F) for 50-90 min until the internal meat temperature reaches 68-70° C (154-158° F).

Cool sausages in cold running water for about 10 min, then hang them up and cool down to below 6°C (43°F).

If smoky flavor is desired, after cooling the sausages may be cold smoked at 18° C (64° F) for 5-6 hours. Store in refrigerator.

Chicken Liver Sausage

Chicken livers are very inexpensive and widely available, however, they can be sometimes slightly bitter. In this recipe the smoked bacon will provide extra flavor.

Chicken livers	300 g	0.66 lb
Lean pork	200 g	0.44 lb
Smoked bacon	300 g	0.66 lb
Pork jowls, pork skins, fresh pork belly	100 g	0.22 lb
Pork trimmings rich in connective tissue	100 g	0.22 b

Ingredients per 1 kg (2.2 lb) of meat

Salt	15 g	2.5 tsp
Pepper	2.0 g	1 tsp
Allspice, ground	1.0 g	1/2 tsp
Marjoram	1.0 g	1/2 tsp
Onion, chopped	40 g	1/2 onion

Fry chopped onion in lard until glassy.

Except liver and smoked bacon cook all meats in hot water at 90° C (195° F) until soft. Drain and cool. Save meat stock.

Grind lean pork, smoked bacon and onions through 1/4" (6 mm) plate.

Grind all other meats and trimmings through 1/8" (3 mm) plate, then emulsify in a food processor with liver and 60 ml of meat stock. Add salt and spices during this step.

Mix ground meat with emulsified paste.

Stuff firmly into 36 mm hog casings.

Cook in water at 80° C (176° F) for 35 minutes. You can combine the remaining meat stock with water.

Cool for 10 minutes in cold water. Dry briefly and refrigerate.

Leverpølse

Danish liver sausage.

Pork liver	300 g	0.66 lb
Veal	300 g	0.66 lb
Pork belly, jowls	200 g	0.44 lb
Back fat	100 g	0.44 lb
Lean pork	100 g	0.22 lb

Ingredients per 1 kg (2.2 lb) of meat

Salt	12 g	2 tsp
White pepper	2.0 g	1 tsp
Marjoram	1.0 g	1/2 tsp
Nutmeg	0.5 g	1/4 tsp
Ginger	0.5 g	1/4 tsp
Thyme	0.5 g	1/4 tsp
Diced onion	50 g	1 small

Simmer veal, lean pork, jowls and belly in hot water until cooked. Save the meat stock.
Chop onion finely and fry in grease until glassy.
Scald liver in hot water for 3 minutes.
Dice back fat into 1/4" (6 mm) cubes.
Slice liver into 1/4" (6 mm) discs.
Grind lean pork, veal, jowls and belly through 1/4" (6 mm) plate.
Emulsify liver in in a food processor.
Add ground meats (except diced back fat), onions, spices and 60 ml (2 oz fl) of meat stock in a food processor.
Emulsify until a smooth paste is obtained.
Pour into a bowl and mix with back fat cubes.
Stuff losely into 36 mm hog casings.
Cook sausages in hot water at 80° C (176° F) for 30 minutes.
Cool in cold water for 10 minutes, then spread on a table to cool.

Note: if back fat cubes are not to be displayed, emulsify back fat with the rest of ingredients in the food processor.
After cooling the sausage can be smoked with a thin smoke at 18° C (64° F) for 2-4 hours.
Refrigerate.

Liver Sausage with Cream
(Sahneleberwurst)

A German liver sausage with sweat cream.

Pork liver	400 g	0.88 lb
Pork belly, jowls, back fat	600 g	1.32 lb

Ingredients per 1 kg (2.2 lb) of meat

Salt	18 g	3 tsp
Pepper	2.0 g	1 tsp
Kardamom	0.5 g	1/4 tsp
Ginger	0.5 g	1/2 tsp
Mace	0.5 g	1/4 tsp
Onion, chopped	40 g	1/2 onion
Cream	60 ml	2 oz fl

Cook pork fats (except liver) in water at 80° C (176° F) until semi-soft. Drain and cool. Grind through 1/8" (3 mm) plate.

Slice the liver into discs and scald for 5 minutes with cold water. Drain and cool. Grind through 1/8" (3 mm) plate.

Fry chopped onion in lard until light yellow, but not brown.

Mix fat, liver, cream and all ingredients together.

Stuff into 40 mm hog casings.

Cook in water at 80° C (176° F) for 40 minutes. Immerse for 10 minutes in cold water. Drain, dry briefly and refrigerate.

Liver Sausage with Semolina
(Kiszka pasztetowa z manną)

Polish liver sausage with semolina.

Pork (butt)	200 g	0.44 lb
Pork or veal liver	250 g	0.55 lb
Fat trimmings	400 g	0.88 lb
Back fat	50 g	0.11 lb
Semolina flour	100 g	0.22 lb

Ingredients per 1 kg (2.2 lb) material

Salt	18 g	3 tsp
Pepper	2.0 g	1 tsp
Marjoram	1.0 g	1/2 tsp
Onion	25 g	1/2 small onion

Cut back fat into 1/4" (5-6 mm) cubes.

Soak liver in cold running water for 1 hour, remove any glands or sinews, cut into slices and place in hot (not boiling) water. Poach at 90°C (194°F) for 8-10 min stirring frequently. Follow the same procedure with diced back fat for 5 min. Then cool liver and back fat pieces in cold water for 5 min and drain.

Cook meats (except fat) at 95° C (203° F) until soft. Save stock.

Grind liver through 1/8" (3 mm) mm plate. Grind pork and fat trimmings through 1/8" (3 mm) plate. Using food processor emulsify semolina adding equal amount of meat stock or water. Add and emulsify liver. Add ground meat, spices and fat trimmings and emulsify together. Mix emulsified mixture with cubes of back fat until uniformly distributed.

Stuff loosely into pork bungs, beef middles or 65 mm cellulose casings. Bungs and middles: 36-50 cm (14-20") long, 4-8 cm (1.5 - 3") thick. Synthetic casings: 40-45 cm (16-18") long, 65 mm dia. The ends tied with a twine.

Immerse sausages into boiling water and cook at 80-85° C (176-185° F) for 50-90 min until sausages reach 68-70° C (154-158° F) internal temperature. Place sausages for 15 minutes in cold water, then hang them up and cool to 6°C (43° F) or lower. Refrigerate.

Liver Sausage with Raisins

Aromatic liver sausage with raisins and nuts.

Pork liver	400 g	0.88 lb
Pork meat trimmings	300 g	0.66 lb
Pork belly, jowls, pork fat trimmings	300 g	0.66 lb

Ingredients per 1 kg (2.2 lb) of meat

Onions	40 g	1/2 small
White bread	60 g	2 oz
Blanched almonds, diced	45 g	1.5 oz
Raisins	45 g	1.5 oz
Currants	60 g	2 oz
Fine sugar	45 g	1.5 oz
Salt	12 g	2 tsp
Cinnamon	0.5 g	1/4 tsp
Nutmeg	0.5 g	1/4 tsp
Cloves, ground	0.3 g	1/8 tsp
Vanilla	5 ml	1 tsp
Milk	60 ml	2 oz fl
Water	60 ml	2 oz fl

Break bread into small pieces and soak in 60 ml of milk.

Dice onions finely and fry them in fat until glassy.

Soak raisins and currants in 60 ml of water.

Cut pork liver into slices, remove the blood veins, any glands and sinews. Scald with hot water until the livers are clean. Grind liver through 1/8" (3 mm) plate.

Cook meats and fat (except liver) in hot water (below the boiling point) for 30 minutes. Drain and cool. Save meat stock.

Grind meats and fat through 1/8" (3 mm) plate.

Emulsify pork liver in food processor.

Take a mixing bowl and mix ground meat and fat, emulsified liver, bread, onions, raisins, almonds, salt, sugar and spices. Add a little water if needed.

Stuff into hog casings, beef rounds or synthetic casings making links 12" (30 cm) long.

Cook in meat stock or in water at 75° C (167° F) for 35 minutes.

Cool sausages in cold water for 10 minutes.

Dry in air and refrigerate

Liver Sausage with Rice-Czech

Liver sausage with rice is a popular sausage in East European countries. Hungarian Hurka, Polish and Czech/Slovak liver sausages are all somewhat similar.

Pork liver	500 g	1.1 lb
Pork belly	200 g	0.44 lb
Rice	250 g	0.55 lb
Onion	50 g	1/2 onion

Ingredients per 1 kg (2.2 lb) of materials

Salt	18 g	3 tsp
Garlic	7 g	2 cloves
White pepper	2 g	1 tsp
Allspice, ground	1 g	1/2 tsp
Marjoram, ground	2 g	1 tsp

Scald liver in hot water for two minutes. Remove, cool with cold water and drain. Add pork belly to the same water and cook until tender. Remove, cool with cold water and drain.

In the same stock cook rice, but do not overcook. Drain rice and save meat stock for cooking sausages.

Grind liver and pork belly through 1/8" (3 mm) plate.

Chop onion finely and fry in lard or oil until glassy.

Mix liver, bacon, onions, salt and spices together.

Stuff loosely (rice may still expand) into 32 mm natural or synthetic casings. Water proof casings are suitable.

Cook for 30 minutes in remaining meat stock or water at 176° F (80° F).

Cool sausages in cold water. Dry briefly and refrigerate.

Salchicha de Higado (*Liver Sausage*)

A basic Spanish liver sausage. Liver sausages can be spreadable, have a firm texture and be of grey, pink, yellow or almost white color. They can include rice, bread, eggs, tripe, cream and flours. Different livers can also be used: veal, pork, rabbit, goose, beef, poultry or wild game.

Lean pork	300 g	0.66 lb
Pork liver	300 g	0.66 lb
Back fat, pork belly, jowls	250 g	0.55 lb
Meat trimmings rich in connective tissue	50 g	0.11 lb
Pork skins	50 g	0.11 lb
Chopped onion	50 g	0.11 lb

Ingredients per 1 kg (2.2 lb) of material

Salt	12 g	2 tsp
White pepper	2.0 g	1 tsp
Allspice	1.0 g	1/2 tsp
Nutmeg	0.5 g	1/4 tsp
Meat stock from cooking meats	60 ml	2 oz fl

Cook pork meat (except liver), meat trimmings and skins in water at 95° C (203° F) until soft. Cook belly, back fat, jowls for 10 minutes only. Drain and cool. Save meat stock.

Fry finely chopped onion in lard until light yellow, but not brown.

Grind meat and fat through 1/4" (6 mm) plate.

Grind liver through 1/8" (3 mm) plate.

Using a food processor emulsify liver, skins and meat trimmings rich in connective tissue adding spices and 60 ml of meat stock.

Mix ground meat, fat and emulsified paste together.

Stuff into 36-40 mm hog casings.

Cook in water at 80° C (176° F) for 40-50 minutes. Immerse for 10 minutes in cold water. Drain, dry briefly and refrigerate.

Notes

Don't cook the liver, just scald it with hot water. Cooked liver loses its emulsifying properties. You can also briefly insert liver in hot water and remove it, repeating the process 3 times. The liver will change color on the outside from dark red to pale.

Blood Sausages

Black Pudding

Black pudding is an English blood sausage. It is often grilled, fried, baked or boiled in its skin though it can be eaten cold as well. Black puddings are also served sliced and fried or grilled as part of a traditional full breakfast in much of the UK and Ireland, a tradition that followed British and Irish emigrants around the world.

British pudding is usually bound with oatmeal and rusk with cubes of fat added. It goes very well with apples, apples stuffed with black pudding, and are tasty and extremely attractive when baked in an oven.

Blood	500 g	1.10 lb
Fat (beef or pork)	250 g	0.55 lb
Oats, barley or both	250 g	0.55 lb

Ingredients per 1 kg (2.2 lb) of material

Salt	18 g	3 tsp
Black pepper	2.0 g	1 tsp
Mace	1.0 g	½ tsp
Ground coriander	2.0 g	1 tsp
Onion, finely chopped	30 g	1 oz

Cook oats in water. Drain. Cut fat into 1/4" (6 mm) cubes. Mix diced fat with blood and other ingredients.

Stuff loosely into 32-36 mm hog casings. Make links 12" (30 cm) long.

Cook in water at 80° C (176° F) for about 40 minutes. Store in refrigerator. The sausage can be eaten cold, fried or baked.

Black Pudding with Cream

An English blood sausage.

Soak oats in water for 30 min. Drain. Cook barley in water for 30 minutes. Drain.

Dice fat into 1/4" (6 mm) cubes. Finely dice onions and fry in a little fat until glassy. Mix with oats and barley. Mix blood with salt, add spices and cream. Pour over barley and oats. Mix all together.

Stuff loosely into 32 - 36 mm hog casings. Cook in water at 80° C (176° F) for about 40 minutes. Store in refrigerator. The sausage can be eaten cold or fried.

Blood	400 g	0.88 lb
Fat (beef or pork)	200 g	0.44 lb
Oats, steel cut	100 g	0.22 lb
Barley	100 g	0.22 lb
Double cream	100 g	3.3 oz fl
Onions	100 g	2 onions

Ingredients per 1 kg (2.2 lb) of materials

Salt	18 g	3 tsp
White pepper	2.0 g	1 tsp
Mace	1.0 g	1/2 tsp
Ground coriander	2.0 g	1 tsp
Cinnamon	1.0 g	1/2 tsp
Onion, finely chopped	30 g	1 oz

Blood Sausage with Bread Crumbs
(Kiszka bułczana krwista)

Polish blood sausage with dried rolls.

Pork head meat	100 g	0.22 lb
Jowls/dewlaps	150 g	0.33 lb
Pork skins, pork lungs,		
pork trimmings	350 g	0.77 lb
Pork blood	200 g	0.44 lb
Dried wheat rolls or		
bread crumbs rolls	200 g	0.44 lb

Limit the amount of skins to no more than 5%, 56 g (2 oz).

Ingredients per 1 kg (2.2 lb) materials

Salt	18 g	3 tsp
Pepper	4.0 g	2 tsp
Marjoram	2.0 g	1 tsp
Allspice	0.5 g	1/4 tsp
Onion	20 g	1/3 onion

Wash meats well in water. Cook meats in a small amount of water:

* heads, lungs, other meats at 80-85° C (176-185° F). Save stock.
* skins at 95°C (203° F) until soft.

After cooking remove gristle from lungs and meat from heads. Spread meats apart on a flat surface to cool.

Grind all meats through 1/8" (3 mm) plate. Soak bread crumbs or dry rolls in 30% (in relation to the weight of the rolls) of left over stock.

Add salt and spices to ground meats and then process in food processor together with blood and soaked rolls.

Stuff into hog casings loosely and form links. Twisted links 3-5" (8-12 cm) each. Form pairs.

Immerse sausages in a boiling water and cook at 80° C (176° F) for 30 min until internal meat temperature reaches 68-70° C (154-158° F).

Place the sausages in cold water for 15 minutes and then spread them on a flat surface to cool.

Refrigerate.

Boudin Noir á la Flamande

Belgian Flemish black pudding.

Pork jowls, pork belly, back fat	400 g	0.88 lb
Pork blood	300 g	10 oz fl
Onions	300 g	0.66 lb
Brown sugar	60 g	2 oz
Raisins, dry	40 g	1.3 oz

Ingredients per 1 kg (2.2 lb) of material

Salt	12 g	2 tsp
Pepper	2.0 g	1 tsp
Cinnamon	1.0 g	1/2 tsp

Simmer meats in hot water until semi-soft. Dice the onions finely and fry in grease on low heat until glassy and golden. Soak raisins in water, then drain.
Grind lean meat through 1/4" (6 mm) plate. Dice fat into 1/4" (6 mm) cubes.
Mix everything together. Stuff into 32 mm hog casings.
Cook in hot water at 80° C (176° F) for 30 minutes. Cool in cold water, dry briefly and refrigerate.

Note: cream is often added. The sausage is usually eaten with applesauce.

Morcela de Arroz

Morcela is a traditional Portuguese and Brazilian black sausage.

Pork trimmings, lean and fat	250 g	0.55 lb
Pork blood	200 ml	0.44 lb
Onions, finely chopped	150 g	0.33 lb
Boiled rice	400 g	0.88 lb

Ingredients per 1 kg (2.2 lb) of material

Salt	12 g	2 tsp
Pepper	2.0 g	1 tsp
Cumin	2.0 g	1 tsp
Cloves, ground.	0.5 g	1/4 tsp
Parsley, chopped	1 sprig	1 tbsp
Red wine	30 ml	1 oz fl

Boil rice but do not overcook. Boil meat and fat trimmings in a little water until soft. Cool and chop into 1/4" (6 mm) pieces. Mix meat, rice, onions and all other ingredients with blood. Stuff into 36-40 mm hog casings. Tie off into rings.
Cook in water at 80° C (176° F) for 35 minutes. Cool and refrigerate.

Morcilla de Burgos

The traditional Morcilla Burgalesa is made without meat. The main ingredients are onions, rice, lard, blood and spices.
The general consensus is that the sausage should be bland, greasy and spicy. Burgos is a city in northern Spain and the historic capital of Castile.

Onions	450 g	0.99 lb
Rice, boiled	200 g	0.44 lb
Lard	200 g	0.44 lb
Pork blood	150 g	0.33 lb

Ingredients per 1 kg (2.2 lb) of material

Salt	12 g	2 tsp
Pepper	2.0 g	1 tsp
Paprika, sweet	10 g	5 tsp
Paprika, hot	10 g	5 tsp
Cayenne	0.5 g	1/4 tsp
Oregano, rubbed	1.0 g	1 tsp
Thyme, rubbed	1.0 g	1 tsp
Cinnamon	0.5 g	1/4 tsp
Cloves, ground	0.2 g	1/8 tsp
Anise, ground	0.2 g	1/8 tsp

Chop the onions finely.
Mix onions with rice, spices and blood. Place lard in pot and apply low heat, stirring often. Whem the lard starts to melt mix it with other ingredients.
Stuff into 36 mm hog casings making rings.
Cook in water at 80° C (176° F) for 30 minutes.
Cool and refrigerate.
To serve, fry in butter or barbecue.

Note: classic morcillas de Burgos are made with the locally grown Horcal onion which is the main ingredient. It is believed that this onion is what gives the sausage its character.

Thüringer Rotwurst

Thüringer Rotwurst has been made in Germany for hundreds of years. It is produced all over the Thuringia region of Germany. Thüringer Rotwurst is known and sought-after far and wide and is also called the 'Queen of Blood Sausages'.

Lean pork: shoulder, leg, head meat, heart	400 g	0.88 lb
Pork belly, jowls	300 g	0.66 lb
Back fat	100 g	0.22 lb
Liver	50 g	0.11 lb
Skins	75 g	2.65 oz
Blood	75 g	2.5 fl oz

Ingredients per 1 kg (2.2 lb) of meat

Salt	18 g	3 tsp
Cure #1	2.5 g	1/2 tsp
Pepper	3.0 g	1.5 tsp
Marjoram	3.0 g	1.5 tsp
Allspice, ground	0.5 g	1/4 tsp
Cloves, ground	0.5 g	1/4 tsp
Onions	30 g	1/2 onion

Cook meat (except liver) in water until soft.
Cook back fat (below the boiling point) in water for 10 minutes.
Cook skins until semi soft. (A thumb should penetrate the skin).
Cut meat into 1/2" (12 mm) cubes.
Cut belly/jowls into 1/4" (6 mm) pieces.
Cut back fat into 1/4" (6 mm) cubes.
Mix meats with salt and cure #1, if not cured previously.
Grind cooked skins, onions and liver through 1/8" (3 mm) plate.
Warm up the blood slightly and mix with ground skins, liver ad spices.
Add meats and fat and mix everything together.
Stuff loosely into large natural or synthetic casings.
Cook in hot water at 80° C (176° F) allowing 10 minutes cooking time for 10 mm (1 cm) casing diameter - 40 mm sausage will be cooked 40 minutes.

Note: Thüringer Rotwurst is characterised by its bright red color. The best color will be developed by curing lean meat with salt and sodium nitrite (cure #1) before cooking. Thüringer Rotwurst carries PGI, 2003 classification.

Tongue Blood Sausage *(Zungenblutwurst)*

German sliceable blood sausage. Tongues should be cured so they will stand out in sliced sausage.

Pork tongue*	500 g	1.10 lb
Pork fat trimmings	200 g	0.44 lb
Pork skins	150 g	0.33 lb
Pork blood	150 g	0.33 lb

Ingredients per 1 kg (2.2 lb of meat

Salt	12 g	2 tsp
Pepper	2.0 g	1 tsp
Allspice, ground	1.0 g	1/2 tsp
Marjoram	3.0 g	2 tsp
Mace	0.5 g	1/4 tsp
Cloves, ground	0.5 g	1/4 tsp
Onions, chopped	30 g	1/3 onion

Boil skins and pork fat trimmings at 80° C (176° F) until soft. Grind when still warm with raw chopped onion through 3 mm (1/8") plate.
Dice the cured tongues* into 25-30 mm (1") cubes.
Mix tongues, ground skins, blood and all ingredients together.
Stuff into 120 mm synthetic waterproof casings making 50 cm (20") sections.
Boil at 80° C (176° F) for 180 minutes.
Immerse in tap water for 15 minutes. Place on a flat surface to cool. Roll over once in a while.
Refrigerate.

Notes:
* curing tongues. Make 40° Salometer brine (10° Baume):
1 gal water, 333 g (0.73 lb) salt; Cure #1, 120 g (4.2 oz). About 3/4 quart (710 ml) of brine is needed for 1 kg of meat. Inject some brine into tongues so they gain about 10% of their original weight and then place them in brine in a suitable container. Hold them completely submerged for 72 hours.
Remove the skin from the tongues, then slice them into thick discs. Boil the tongues at 90° C (194° F) for about 2 hours. Cool the tongues under running water.

Head Cheeses

Cabeza de Jabalí

The Spanish word jabalí signifies in English "wild boar", so it may be assumed that wild boar head meat was used in the past. Cabeza de Jabalí is a Spanish head cheese belonging to the "fiambre" group of meat products. It is made from pork head meat, ears, snouts, lips, jowls, skins, tongue and is basically a head cheese (queso de cabeza). Cabeza de Jabalí is listed in the Spanish Official Government Meat Standards Bulletin (Boletín Oficial del Estado, Real Decreto 474/2014, 13th June) as the product made from pork head meat. When sliced, or formed in a mold as meat jelly, it offers a wonderful display of different meat cuts which are held together by a natural aspic (jelly). In addition to different cuts of meat which come in different colors, for better visual effects decorative items such as red bell pepper, olives, sliced lemon or pistachios are locked in gelatin creating an interesting display.

Pork head meat*	400 g	0.88 lb
Pork jowls	300 g	0.66 lb
Meat trimmings, ears, snouts	200 g	0.44 lb
Pork skins	100 g	0.22 lb

Ingredients per 1 kg (2.2 lb) of meat

Salt	18 g	3 tsp
Pepper, white	4.0 g	2 tsp
Cumin	2.0 g	1 tsp
Garlic, diced	3.5 g	1 clove
Meat stock	100 ml	3.3 oz fl

Cook meats in a small amount of water: pork heads at 85°C (185°F), and pork skins at 95°C (203°F) until soft. Add soup greens for better flavor. Spread meats on a flat surface to cool. Save meat stock. Separate meat from bones when still warm.

Cut meat into smaller pieces, cut skins into short strips. Mix all meats with spices adding 10% of meat stock in relation to the weight of pork heads with bones. The meat stock is the result of boiling meats.

Stuff mixture loosely into hog stomachs or beef bungs about 12" (30 cm) long. Cook in water at 82°C (180°F) for 90-150 min (depending on size) until the internal temperature of the meat reaches 154-158°F (68-70°C). Remove air with a needle from pieces that swim up to the surface.

Spread head cheeses on a flat surface at 2-6°C (35-43°F) and let the steam out. Place sausages between two boards and place heavy weight on the top. Leave undisturbed for 12 hours at cool temperature. After cooling clean head cheeses of any fat and aspic that accumulated on the surface. Store in refrigerator.

Notes
Head cheese was traditionally made with pork head meat, however, a person a city will find it hard to get a pork or wild boar head. What is needed is meat that is rich in connective tissue; picnic (front leg), hocks, feet, skin are great gelatin producers.

Italian Head Cheese
(Salceson włoski)

Although carrying an Italian name, this has been always a very popular head cheese in Poland.

Pork heads	750 g	1.65 lb
Meat from beef heads	130 g	0.28 lb
Pork skins	120 g	0.26 lb

Meat from beef heads may be replaced with beef meat or boned and cured pork picnics.

Ingredients per 1 kg (2.2 lb.) of meat

Salt	18 g	3 tsp
Cure # 1	2.5 g	1/2 tsp
Pepper	2.0 g	1 tsp
Caraway	1.0 g	1/2 tsp
Garlic	3.5 g	1 clove

Cook meats in a small amount of water: pork heads at 85° C (185° F), beef head meat and pork skins at 95° C (203° F). Remove meat from heads and spread all meats apart on a flat surface to cool. Save meat stock.

- cut pork head meat into strips ⅝ x ¾" (1.5 x 2 cm) by 2 x 4" (7-10 cm)
- cut beef head meat into strips ⅜ x 2" (1 x 5 cm)
- grind other meats with 1/8" (3 mm) plate.

Mix meats with salt, cure # 1, spices and 10% of the meat stock (in relation to the weight of the meat).
Stuff *loosely* into pork stomachs, bladders or 100 mm synthetic strong casings.
Flattened pork stomachs, 30 cm (12") long, about
20 cm (8") wide and 8 cm (3") high.
Cook in water at 82 °C (180° F) for 90-150 min (depending on size) until meat reaches 68-70° C (154-158° F) internal temperature. Remove air with a needle from pieces that swim up to the surface.
Spread head cheeses on a flat surface and let the steam out. Flatten stomachs with weight and cool to 6° C (43° F).
Clean head cheeses of any fat and aspic that accumulated on the surface, even them out and cut off excess twine. Keep refrigerated.

Note: * it is not expected that animal heads will be cured in home production, however, you can cure raw meats with salt and cure #1 (see dry curing method in Chapter 1) before the meats are submitted to cooking if you want the head cheese to contain red cuts.

Queso de Cabeza
(Head cheese)

Argentinian head cheese.

Pork head, leg meat, pork skins, snouts, meats with connective tissue	1000 g	2.2 lb

Ingredients per 1 kg (2.2 lb) of meat

Salt	15 g	2.5 tsp
Peppercorns	4.0 g	2 tsp
Cayenne	1.0 g	1/2 tsp
Onion	60 g	2 oz
Garlic	10 g	3 cloves
Bay leaf	1 leaf	1
Celery	1 stalk	1
Leek	1 stalk	1
Parsnip	1 root	1
Carrot	1 root	1
Oregano, rubbed	10 g	1 Tbsp
White wine	60 ml	2 oz fl

Place all meats in a suitable pot, add leek, celery, parsnip, carrot, onion, peppercorns and cover with 1 inch of water and wine. Bring to a boil and simmer below boiling point until meats are soft and the bones are easily removable.

Drain the meats, spread on the table and allow to cool. Save meat stock, discard vegetables.

When the meats are still warm, separate the meat from the bones. Cut larger chunks into smaller pieces, sut the skins into strips.

Mix meats with salt, garlic, oregano, cayenne adding about 1/2 cup (125 ml) of the meat stock. This meat stock is a naturally produced gelatin.

Using a ladle stuff the mixture loosely into pork stomachs or large diameter synthetic casings.

Cook in water at 82° C (180° F) for 90-120 min (depending on the size) until meat reaches 68-70° C (154-158° F) internal temperature.

Spread head cheeses on a flat surface and let the steam out. Flatten with weight and cool to 6° C (43° F) or lower.

Clean head cheeses of any fat and aspic that accumulated on the surface and cut off excess twine.

Keep refrigerated. Eat cold with a roll and lemon juice or vinegar.

Souse

American head cheese. Souse also known as Sulz is a head cheese to which vinegar has been added. It is a jellied meat sausage that is stuffed in a large diameter casing or simply made as a jellied meat loaf. As most people add vinegar or squeeze some lemon juice into head cheese when eating it, so it should not be a surprise that producers add vinegar (5%) into the mix. This also contributes positively towards a longer shelf life of the product as acidity inhibits the growth of bacteria.

Pork head meat, jowls, skins, tongues, hearts, meat trimmings ....450 g 0.99 lb
Pigs feet .... 300 g   0.66 lb
Meat broth
(from cooking meat) ...... 200 g   0.48 lb
Vinegar, 5% .... 50 g   0.11 lb

Ingredients per 1 kg (2.2 lb) of material

Salt	18 g	3 tsp
Pepper	2.0 g	1 tsp
Bay leaf	1 leaf	1
Garlic	3.5 g	1 clove
Cumin	1.0 g	1/2 tsp

Place meats, salt, pepper, bay leaf and spices in a pot and cover with about two inches of water. Cover and cook below the boiling point for about 2 hours or until meat separates easily from bones. Strain and save meat stock for later. Separate meats from bones. It is easier to perform this task when meats are still warm.
Cut meats into smaller pieces.
Mix meats with meat stock, vinegar and smashed garlic.
Now you can go two different ways:
1. Pour your souse into containers, let them sit for 2 hours at room temperature and then place in a refrigerator. Keep it there for 12 hours to give the souse time to set. Serve in containers. *OR*
2. Stuff with a ladle into pork stomachs or large diameter waterproof casings, tie the ends and cook in water at 85° C (185° F). Cool partially in cold water and place at room temperature for about 2 hours for gelatin to set. Place for 12 hours into refrigerator before cutting.

Note: green peppers, pimentos or pickles are often added to souse to make it visually attractive.

White Head Cheese Supreme
(Salceson biały wyborowy)

A popular Polish head cheese.

Pork heads	750 g	1.65 lb
Beef head meat	130 g	0.28 lb
Pork skins	120 g	0.26 lb

Ingredients per 1 kg (2.2 lb) of meat

Salt	18 g	3 tsp
Cure # 1	2.0 g	1/2 tsp
Pepper	1.0 g	1/2 tsp
Caraway	0.5 g	1/4 tsp
Garlic	1.5 g	1/2 clove

Cook until soft in small amount of water:

*   heads at 85° C (185° F)
*   skins at 95° C (203° F)

Remove warm meat from heads and spread apart on a flat surface to cool. Spread skins and let them cool.

Cut pork head meat into strips 3-4" (7-10 cm) x ½-¾" (1-1.5 cm). Cut beef head meat into strips ½" (1 cm) wide and 2" (5 cm) long. Grind skins and any meat with sinews through 1/8" (3 mm) plate.

Mix meat with salt, cure #1, spices and 10% of the meat stock (in relation to the weight of the meat).

Stuff loosely into stomach, bladder or 100 mm synthetic strong casings. Flattened pork or beef bladders in a shape of irregular disk up to 10" (25 cm) diameter and 3" (8 cm) thick.

Cook in water at 82° C (180° F) for 90-150 min (depending on size) until the internal temperature of the meat reaches 68-70° C (154-158° F). Remove air with a needle from pieces that swim up to the surface.

Spread head cheeses on a flat surface and let the steam out. Flatten stomachs with weight and cool to 6°C (43°F) or less.

Clean head cheeses of any fat and aspic that accumulated on the surface, even them out and cut off excess twine.

Fermented Sausages

Chorizo de Cantipalos

This classic dry chorizo originates in the municipality of Cantipalos in the province of Segovia of the autonomous region de Castilla y León in the middle of Spain. For hundreds of years the area of Cantipalos was highly regarded for making sausages, but 1900 is the date which is credited as the official beginning of the sausage making industry in Cantipalos. By 1928 the sausages from Cantipalos were regularly shipped (packed in cans) to Mexico and other countries. From 2011 Chorizo de Cantipalos carries a protective geographical indication certificate (PGI). Chorizo de Cantimpalos is a cured sausage product made from fresh fatty pork, with salt and pimentón as basic ingredients, to which garlic and oregano may also be added, and subjected to a drying and maturing process.

Lean pork	700 g	1.54 lb
Back fat or		
hard fat trimmings	300 g	0.66 lb

Ingredients per 1 kg (2.2 lb) of meat

Sea salt, finely ground	22 g	4 tsp
Pimentón de la Vera, sweet	20 g	3.5 Tbsp
Pimentón de la Vera, hot	2.0 g	1 tsp
Oregano, rubbed	0.2 g	1/4 tsp
Garlic, diced	4.0 g	1.5 cloves

For chorizos *sarta* and *achorizado* grind meat through 10-16 mm (3/8-1/2") plate.
For chorizos *cular* style grind meat through 18-26 mm (3/4-1") plate.
Mix salt, spices and meats together. Hold for 12-36 hours in refrigerator.
Stuff into natural casings:

- 34-40 mm pork ring shaped casings (***sarta*** style), the ends tied together.
- a string of several chorizo sausages (***achorizado*** ristra style) about 12 cm (5") long, 36-50 mm in diameter, tied or wired together with ends connected together with twine forming a long U-shaped loop.
- pork bungs (***cular*** style) of more than 38 mm in diameter, an irregular cylindrical shape straight sections.

Dry at 6-16° C (43-60° F), 60-85% humidity for 1/2 of the total drying time.
Dry at 12-15° C (57-59° F), 60-80% humidity for the remaining drying time.

- *sarta* style - total drying time 21 days.
- *achorizado* ristra style - total drying time 24 days.
- *cular* - total drying time up to 40 days.

Store at 10-12° C (50-52° F), 60-70% humidity.

Notes
The sausage develops a thin white mold.
The sausage is finished when it loses about 30% of its original weight.

Metka
(Metka)

Metka is a cold smoked spreadable sausage that is related to German Mettwurst. Metka sausages were not cooked and this why they were less popular in summer months. With the advent of refrigeration the storing problem has been eliminated. *This cold smoked spreadable sausage recipe comes from the official Polish Government archives.*

Pork (butt, picnic)		600 g	1.32 lb
Beef		400 g	0.88 lb

Ingredients per 1 kg (2.2 lb.) of meat

Salt	21 g	3.5 tsp
Cure #1	2.5 g	1/2 tsp
Pepper	1.0 g	1/2 tsp
Paprika	1.0 g	1/2 tsp
Sugar	2.0 g	1/2 tsp

Curing: cut all meat into 5-6 cm (2") cubes, mix with salt and cure #1. Keep pork and beef separate. Pack tightly in containers and cover with a clean cloth. Hold in cooler at 4-6° C (40-42° F) for 72 hours. Grind all meats through 1/8" (3 mm) plate. Re-freeze and grind again. Mix meats until sticky. During mixing add remaining ingredients.

Stuff firmly into 36-40 mm beef rounds, cellulose or fibrous casings. Hang for 1-2 days at 2-6° C (35-43° F) and 85-90% humidity. Apply cold smoke at 18-22° C (64-72° F) for 1-2 days until casings develop brown redddish color. Cool in air to 12° C (53° F) or lower. Store in refrigerator.

Mettwurst-Braunschweiger

German spreadable sausage.

Beef		300 g	0.66 lb
Pork butt		300 g	0.66 lb
Pork belly		400 g	0.88 lb

Ingredients per 1 kg (2.2 lb) of meat

Salt	24 g	4 tsp
Cure #1	2.5 g	1/2 tsp
Dextrose	2.0 g	1/2 tsp
Pepper	2.5 g	1 tsp
Paprika	1.0 g	1/2 tsp
Mace	1.0 g	1/2 tsp
Juniper extract*	1.0 g	1/4 tsp
T-SPX culture	0.12 g	use scale

Grind all meats through 1/8" (3 mm) plate. Re-freeze meats and grind again twice. You may grind once and then emulsify in the food processor without adding water.
Add all ingredients, starter culture included. Stuff firmly into 40-60 mm beef middles or fibrous casings. Form 8-10" (20-25 cm) links. Ferment for 48 hours at 18° C (64° F), 75% humidity. Apply cold smoke for 12 hours at 18° C (64° F). Store in a refrigerator.

* insert 20 g of crushed juniper berries into 120 ml (½ cup) vodka or cognac and leave in a closed jar for 2-3 days. Filter the liquid from the berries.

Pepperoni

The term "pepperoni" is a borrowing of peperoni, the plural of peperone, the Italian word for bell pepper. Traditional pepperoni is a dry sausage, smoked, air dried, sometimes cooked. Pepperoni can be made from beef, pork or a combination such as 30% beef and 70% pork. Pepperoni is a lean sausage with fat content < 30%. Cheaper, fast-fermented (semi-dry) and cooked types end up as toppings to pizzas worldwide to give flavor. Traditionally made Italian pepperoni was not smoked.

Pork	700 g	1.54 lb
Beef	300 g	0.66 lb

Ingredients per 1 kg (2.2 lb) of meat

Salt	28 g	5 tsp
Cure #2	2.5 g	1/2 tsp
Dextrose	2.0 g	1/3 tsp
Sugar	3.0 g	1/2 tsp
Black pepper	3.0 g	1.5 tsp
Paprika	6.0 g	3 tsp
Anise (or fennel) seeds, cracked	2.5 g	2 tsp
Cayenne pepper	2.0 g	1 tsp
T-SPX culture	0.12 g	use scale

Grind pork and beef through 3/16" plate (5 mm).
Mix all ingredients with meat.
Stuff firmly into beef middles or 2" fibrous casings.
Ferment at 20° C (68° F) for 72 hours, 90-85% humidity.
Optional step: cold smoke for 8 hours (<22° C, 72° F).
Dry at 16-12° C (60-54° F), 85-80% humidity. In about 6-8 weeks a shrink of 30% should be achieved.
Store sausages at 10-15° C (50-59° F), <75% humidity.

Salami - Hungarian

The Hungarian salami is a unique sausage which is smoked and has a white mold. In the traditional process the use of starter cultures and sugars are not allowed. The sausage should not exhibit any acidity. The recipe below contains very little dextrose (sugar), just to provide a margin of safety during the first stage of fermentation.

Lean pork	800 g	1.76 lb
Back fat or		
hard fat trimmings	200 g	0.44 lb

Ingredients per 1 kg (2.2 lb) of meat

Salt	28 g	5 tsp
Cure #2	2.5 g	1/2 tsp
Dextrose (glucose)	2.0 g	1/2 tsp
White pepper	3.0 g	1.5 tsp
Paprika	6.0 g	3 tsp
Garlic powder	2.0 g	1 tsp
OR fresh garlic	7.0 g	2 cloves
Tokay wine		
(Hungarian sweet wine)	15 ml	1 Tbsp
T-SPX culture	0.12 g	use scale

Grind pork and back fat through 3/16" plate (5 mm).
30 minutes before mixing dissolve starter culture in 1 tablespoon de-chlorinated water.
Mix all ingredients with ground meat.
Stuff firmly into beef middles or 3" protein lined fibrous casings.
Ferment at 20° C (68° F) for 72 hours, 90-85% humidity.
Cold smoke for 4 days (<22° C, 72° F). You can apply smoke during the 2nd stage of fermentation.
Dry at 16-12° C (60-54° F), 85-80% humidity for 2-3 months.
Store sausages at 10-15° C (50-59° F), <75% humidity.

Salami Milano

Salami Milano and Salami Genoa are very similar, however, they incorporate different proportions of raw materials. Some typical combinations: 50/30/20 (this recipe), 40/40/20 or 40/30/30. Salami Genoa is also known as Salami di Alessandra. Salami Milano is chopped somewhat finer than Salami Genoa.

Lean pork trimmings (ham, butt)	500 g	1.10 lb
Beef (chuck)	300 g	0.66 lb
Pork back fat or hard fat trimmings	200 g	0.44 lb

Ingredients per 1 kg (2.2 lb) of meat

Salt	28 g	5 tsp
Cure #2	2.5 g	1/2 tsp
Dextrose (glucose)	2.0 g	1/2 tsp
Sugar	3.0 g	1/2 tsp
White pepper	3.0 g	1.5 tsp
Garlic powder	1.0 g	1/2 tsp
OR fresh garlic	3.5 g	1 clove
T-SPX culture	0.12 g	use scale

Grind pork and back fat through 3/16" plate (5 mm). Grind beef with 1/8" (3 mm) plate.

30 minutes before mixing dissolve starter culture in 1 tablespoon de-chlorinated water.

Mix all ingredients with ground meat.

Stuff firmly into 80 mm protein lined fibrous casings. Make 25" long links.

Ferment at 20° C (68° F) for 72 hours, 90-85% humidity.

Dry at 16-12° C (60-54° F), 85-80% humidity for 2-3 months until the sausage loses around 30-35% in weight.

Store sausages at 10-15° C (50-59° F), 75% humidity.

Note: if mold is desired spray with Mold 600 culture after stuffing.

The following spice and herb combination can be found in some recipes:

spices: 4 parts coriander, 3 parts mace, 2 parts allspice, 1 part fennel.

herbs: 3 parts marjoram, 1 part thyme, 1 part basil.

Some recipes ask for the addition of red wine and you may add around 30 ml (1 oz fl).

Salchichón de Vic

After chorizo, salchichón is the second most popular dry sausage in Spain. The black pepper is the principal spice used, pimentón *is not added* to salchichon. Technically speaking, salchichón may be considered to be the Spanish equivalent of Italian salami.

The first references written about sausage from Vic date back to 1456. In the past this product was produced in the farms located in the Plana de Vic taking advantage of the suitable climate conditions of the area. Salchichón de Vic also known as Llonganissa de Vic is made in the province of Barcelona. Salchichón de Vic carries PGI, 2001 classification.

Lean pork (shoulder, leg)	800 g	1.76 lb
Pork belly	150 g	0.33 lb
Back fat	50 g	0.11 lb

Ingredients per 1 kg (2.2 lb) of meat

Salt	25 g	4 tsp
Sugar	3.0 g	1/2 tsp
White pepper	3.0 g	1.5 tsp
Black pepper, whole	1.0 g	1 tsp

Dice back fat into 6 mm (1/4") cubes.
Grind meats through 8 mm (3/8") plate.
Mix ground meats with all ingredients.
Hold for 24-48 hours at 4-6° C (40-43° F) or in refrigerator.
Stuff firmly into pork bungs, 50-60 cm (20-24") long.
Ferment/dry at 20° C (68° F) for 48 hours, 90-95% humidity.
Dry at 15→ 12° C (59-54° F), 80 → 75% humidity for 45 days (or longer depending on a diameter of the casing). The sausage is dried until around 30% in weight is lost. The sausage should develop a white mold which is expected and desired.
Store sausages at 10-12° C (50-53° F), <70% humidity.

Notes
Consume raw.
In traditional production the fermentation step was often skipped and the stuffed sausage was only dried for 5-11 months at room temperatures, depending on the diameter of the casing.
Salchichón de Vic, fuet and secallona are Catalan dry sausages that employ similar materials and ingredients, they also follow the same manufacturing steps. Fermenting and drying times will be shorter for fuet and secallona as they are stuffed into smaller diameter casings. Another difference is that secallona is formed into U-shaped loop and salchichón and fuet are straight sections sausages.

Saucisson aux Noisettes *(Dry Sausage with Hazelnuts)*

Because of their wonderful flavor hazelnuts are used to produce such famous products like Nutella™ spread or Ferrero Rocher™ chocolates. When mixed with meat hazelnuts release their aroma during the drying period creating a wonderful dry sausage. Hazelnuts have strong antioxidant properties and are excellent for health.

Lean pork, no connective tissue	750 g	1.65 lb
Back fat or hard fat trimmings	100 g	0.22 lb
Hazelnuts	150 g	0.33 lb

Ingredients per 1 kg (2.2 lb) of materials

Salt	28 g	4.5 tsp
Cure #2	2.5 g	1/2 tsp
Dextrose	2.0 g	1/2 tsp
Sugar	3.0 g	1/2 tsp
Pepper	2.0 g	1 tsp
Nutmeg	1.0 g	1/2 tsp
Cinnamon	0.5 g	1/4 tsp
Cloves	0.25 g	1/8 tsp
T-SPX culture	0.12 g	use scale

Grind lean meat into 3/8" (8 mm) particles.
Cut partially frozen back fat into 1/4 (6 mm) cubes.
Dissolve starter culture in 1 tablespoon de-chlorinated water.
Mix ground meats with salt and cure #2 until sticky. Add spices, culture, whole hazelnuts, chopped fat and mix again.
Stuff firmly into 60 mm pork bungs forming sections 20-30 cm (8-12") long.
Ferment at 20° C (68° F) for 72 hours, 90-85% humidity.
Dry at 16 → 12° C (60-54° F), 85 → 80% humidity for 30 days. The sausage is dried until around 30% in weight is lost.
Store sausages at 10-15° C (50-59° F), <75% humidity.

Note: replacing hazelnuts with walnuts creates another dry sausage:
Saucisson aux Noix *(Dry Sausage with Walnuts)*

Saucisson d'Alsace

A French dry sausage from Alsace region.

Lean pork	800 g	1.76 lb
Back fat	200 g	0.44 lb

Ingredients per 1 kg (2.2 lb) of meat

Salt	28 g	5 tsp
Cure #2	2.5 g	1/2 tsp
Dextrose	2 g	1/2 tsp
Non-fat dry milk	20 g	3 tsp
White pepper	3 g	1.5 tsp
Garlic	2 g	1/2 clove
Nutmeg	0.5 g	1/2 tsp
Cloves, ground	0.3 g	1/4 tsp
Cinnamon	0.5 g	1/2 tsp
Dark rum	15 ml	1 Tbsp
T-SPX culture	0.12 g	use scale

Grind pork and back fat through 3/16" plate (5 mm).
30 minutes before mixing dissolve starter culture in 1 tablespoon de-chlorinated water.
Mix all ingredients with ground meat.
Stuff firmly into beef middles or 3" protein lined fibrous casings.
Ferment at 20° C (68° F) for 60 hours, 90-85% humidity.
Cold smoke at 18-22° C (64-72° F) 12 hours.
Dry at 16-12° C (60-54° F), 85-80% humidity for 1-2 months.
Store sausages at 10-15° C (50-59° F), <75% humidity.

Sobrasada de Mallorca

Sobrasada de Mallorca carries a Protective Geographical Indication certificate (PGI 1996). The sausage must meet the following requirements: lean pork (30-60%), back fat (40-70%), pimentón (4-7%), salt (1.8-2.8%), spices: pepper, rosemary, thyme, oregano. Sobrasada is a very popular sausage in Balearic Islands. As the name implies this sausage originates in the island of Majorca.

Sobrasada includes a lot of pimentón - when made with sweet pimentón only it is known as sweet sobrasada ("dulce") and when hot pimentón is added it becomes hot sobrasada ("picante").

Pork, lean	380 g	0.83 lb
Pork belly	270 g	0.59 lb
Back fat, fat trimmings	350 g	0.77 lb

Ingredients per 1 kg (2.2 lb) of meat

Salt	24 g	4 tsp
White pepper	2.0 g	1 tsp
Pimentón, sweet*	48 g	7 Tbsp
Thyme, ground	2.0 g	2 tsp
Oregano, ground	2.0 g	2 tsp

Grind meat and fat through 5 mm (1/4 tsp).
Mix ground meat and fat with salt and spices. Hold in refrigerator for 24 hours.
Stuff into 40-100 mm pork casings.
Dry at 15-18° C (59-64° F), 75-80% humidity for 30-45 days depending on the diameter of the sausage.
Store at 10-12° C (50-53° F), 60-65% humidity or refrigerate.

Notes
* Although Pimentón de La Vera is the highest quality pimentón it is, however, made from smoked peppers and *must not be added* to Sobrasada de Mallorca in order not to introduce the smoky flavor.
Neither *garlic* nor *sugar* is added to Sobrasada de Mallorca.
Majorcan Sobrasada is traditionally served on bread and topped with variety of spreads such as honey, sugar or apricot jam.
For hot version add 6 g (1 Tbsp) of hot pimentón.

Index

S

T

Printed in Great Britain
by Amazon

18078215R00098